# ECONOMICS IN THE CURRICULUM

# Economics in the Curriculum

---

Developmental Economic Education Program

---

*James D. Calderwood*
*John D. Lawrence*
*John E. Maher*

John Wiley & Sons, Inc.

NEW YORK • LONDON • SYDNEY • TORONTO

Copyright © 1970 by John Wiley & Sons, Inc.

1 2 3 4 5 6 7 8 9 10

Library of Congress Catalog Card Number: 71-107589

Paper: SBN 471 44685 8 (cloth)
471 44686 6 (paper)

PRINTED IN THE UNITED STATES OF AMERICA.

# Foreword

THE FIRST EDITION of this teacher's guide appeared in 1964 at the beginning of the Joint Council's Developmental Economic Education Program (DEEP). We stated then that revisions would be made as the experience of school systems and Affiliated Councils on Economic Education, plus the Joint Council's research, demonstrated new and more effective ways of teaching economics. We now offer this first revision which reflects the experience gained by 30 major school systems engaged in DEEP.

This revision eliminates the previous section on business education which will appear in a separate publication. It includes an additional section on economics at the twelfth grade level. It, also, includes the *Report of the National Task Force on Economic Education in the Schools.*

Greater flexibility in usage by teachers has been achieved by grouping economic ideas by blocks of grades at the elementary level and by placing illustrative examples under five economic topics at the junior-senior high level.

This new arrangement conforms to teaching patterns practiced in most classrooms. Moreover, a cumulative sequence of learning experiences is now more clearly described.

The Joint Council wishes to acknowledge its debt to its Affiliated Councils, the scores of school districts and their teachers, DEEP coordinators, university consultants and participants in the 1964 Princeton conference.

We extend to all school systems and their faculties an invitation to send us their suggestions for future revision of this publication.

*M. L. Frankel, President*
*Joint Council on Economic Education*

January 1970

# *Preface*

---

Is IT IMPORTANT to know something about the social forces over which an informed citizenry can exert influence, thereby helping to shape their destiny? If the answer is yes, then it is important to know something about economics.

Everyone faces economic problems at two levels—the personal and the social. Each day we make economic decisions in the market place on matters affecting our personal lives: we decide what to buy, how much to save, and whether to change jobs; we pay taxes, borrow money, vote at union meetings, make business decisions, and choose between putting our savings in life insurance or in the stock market. For better or worse, these decisions will affect our pocketbook, our happiness, and our future welfare.

We also make economic decisions in the voting booth that affect the society of which we are a part; for example, we vote for or against a school-bond issue; we support candidates for local, state, and federal offices on the basis of their opinions on such issues as labor-management relations, foreign aid, taxes, social security programs, zoning laws, federal aid to education, and urban renewal.

A fundamental assumption of our society has been that voters can make intelligent decisions on these complicated economic issues, but more than half of our high school graduates do not go to college and of those who do many do not study economics. It is evident, therefore, if we wish everyone to have some understanding of this subject that our nation's schools must provide it.

If we accept the idea that economic understanding should be part of the intellectual equipment of high school graduates, two important questions must be answered. First, what should high school graduates know about economics as they prepare to go out into the world—what are the minimum economic understandings for responsible citizenship? Second, how can these understandings, once identified, be introduced into the curriculum? Part One of this teacher's guide responds to the first question and Part Two contains suggested outlines to help teachers decide the second question.

One important source of the economic ideas included in this book is *Economic Education in the Schools: A Report of the National Task Force.* In this report, for the first time, the economics profession, through its official organization, the American Economic Association, indicates the minimum understanding of economics essential for good citizenship and attainable by high school students. The report was a pioneering effort that constituted a landmark in the history of economic education and has been of immense use to all who work in this field.

After the appearance of the report two tasks became necessary. First, the economic concepts mentioned in that document had to be further developed so that teachers might strengthen their own understanding of economics. Second, the concepts had to be related to existing curricula in such a manner that practical classroom application became possible.

The present revised guide attempts these two tasks: Part One contains further development and explanation of the basic economic concepts and Part Two offers illustrations of classroom applications.

Among the important changes in this revision are (a) an emphasis on the use of proved classroom materials gathered from schools in the Developmental Economic Education Program (DEEP); (b) an emphasis on the cohesive perspective that is economics rather than the innumerable applications of the discipline.

The authors are indebted to Robert L. Darcy of Colorado State University, Percy L. Guyton, Jacksonville University, Lawrence Senesh, University of Colorado, Edwin Fenton, Carnegie—Mellon University, Roman F. Warmke, Ohio University, S. Stowell Symmes, Joint Council on Economic Education, Philmore Wass, Connecticut Joint Council on Economic Education, David Meyers, Brookline High School, Brookline, Mass., and Robert Lekachman, State University of New York at Stony Brook, for their help with the original and revised edition of this book.

*James D. Calderwood*
UNIVERSITY OF SOUTHERN CALIFORNIA

*John D. Lawrence*
SONOMA STATE COLLEGE

*John E. Maher*
JOINT COUNCIL ON ECONOMIC EDUCATION

# Contents

# Economic Ideas Every High School Graduate Should Understand

The National Task Force* has identified seven major areas of modern economics that it believes every high school graduate should understand.

1. What economics is all about, why it is important, and how to think about economic problems.
2. The nature of the persistent economic problems faced by all societies: wants, scarce resources, the need for decision making, and the need for an economic system.
3. The market economy of the United States: how it is decided in the United States today (a) what goods and services will be produced, (b) how they will be produced, (c) what total level of production will be maintained, and (d) how what is produced will be shared by the American people.
4. Economic growth and stability: the long- and short-run performance of the American economy pertaining to (a) economic growth—the long-run problems associated with increasing total production of goods and services faster than the rate of population growth so that living standards can rise; (b) economic stability—the determinants of the level of income and employment in the short run or how to manage our economy so that we can have full employment without inflation.
5. The distribution of income: the factors determining the distribution of income among individuals and groups in the United States and thus who will get the goods and services produced.
6. The United States in the world economy: the importance of world trade and finance to the United States and the ways in which the achievement of our economic goals is related to world economic developments.
7. Other economic systems: how other societies organize economic life to achieve their economic goals—not only the communist countries but also the democratic societies of the West and the developing nations of Asia, Africa, and Latin America.

*Economic Education in the Schools, Report of the National Task Force on Economic Education, Committee for Economic Development, September 1961.

# PART ONE

---

# ECONOMIC IDEAS
# AND CONCEPTS

*James D. Calderwood*

# 1

## The Importance of Economics and the Nature of Economic Understanding

### Why Economics Is Important

"EVERYONE must to some extent act as his own economist—in his private life and as a citizen—and both he and the community will be better served if he is well informed and can think clearly and objectively about economic questions." *Task Force Report,* p. 161.

A knowledge of economics is important if we are to meet our responsibilities as citizens and as participants in a complex private enterprise economy.

Individuals have to deal with a multitude of economic problems affecting their own personal lives—how to spend their incomes and what to do with their savings. A knowledge of economics is helpful in this respect. Citizens should also understand the consequences of their economic actions. This much we surely owe to the society of which we are a part.

As citizens, all persons have to make decisions on a wide variety of economic problems of local, state, national, and international significance and then express their views in the voting booth. These problems range all the way from voting on a school-bond issue to making up one's mind about foreign aid, poverty problems, or labor-management relations. Some knowledge of economics is essential if these decisions are to be made intelligently. In this respect economic understanding is part of the basic fabric of a democratic society.

Training in economic analysis, as in mathematics and biology, develops the capacity of a young person to think objectively and rationally. It thus helps his general mental growth.

### What Economics Is and What It Is Not

"The most important step toward understanding in economics—as in

3

other branches of knowledge—is the replacement of emotional, unreasoned judgments by objective rational analysis." *Task Force Report,* p. 161.

Economics is not the same as personal finance. Although the consumer plays a vital role in the economy, an exclusive devotion to "wise buying" or how to open a savings account is not in itself "economics." A study of the behavior of the consumer is only part of the whole.

Economics is concerned with all of society and with the activities of the various groups and institutions it contains—consumers, businessmen, farmers, workers, savers, investors, corporations, and federal, state, and local government. It is a *social* science.

Economics is concerned not only with the individual parts of our economy—the consumer, the business, the union, and the market for a particular product (which we call microeconomics)—but also with the sum of these parts that together constitute the economic system of a country; that is, how the individual parts relate to form a whole. Economics is also concerned with the functioning of the economy, with how fast it is growing, and how vulnerable it is to inflation or depression (which we call macroeconomics).

Although many economic concepts can be understood by reference to personal experiences or through role-playing (e.g., being a consumer), real economic understanding requires an ability to reason abstractly and to consider society as a whole rather than the individual's position in it.

Economics is not just a study of current events and the weighing of the pros and cons of an issue in the morning newspaper. It is a scientific method by which a problem is defined and analyzed in a rational way and by which goals, the alternative ways of reaching them, and the consequences of following each possible line of action, are identified.

To have economic understanding does not mean that "facts" have been memorized. It means that certain "ways of thinking" about economic problems—a scientific method comparable to that involved in physics or chemistry, which permits a rational choice among alternatives—have been acquired. The real test of economic understanding is whether we have the ability to deal with economic problems as they arise in an organized, scientific way. A great economist, John Maynard Keynes, once wrote:

"The theory of economics does not furnish a body of settled conclusions immediately applicable to policy. It is a method rather than a doctrine, an apparatus of the mind, a technique of thinking, which helps its possessor to draw correct conclusions."

Thus the heart of economics is the awareness of and ability to use a set of analytical tools called economic theory. In this respect economics is no different from other disciplines. It is a social *science*.

Economics is not concerned merely with static situations—with how institutions are functioning at this moment alone—but with the dynamics of change and adjustment to change; for example, in economics we study the ways in which prices are determined by supply and demand, the processes of growth, and the problems that are a result of the changes associated with growth over a period of time.

Economists are concerned with value judgments but not with making them. Both personal goals and broader social objectives are, of course, important. Rational choices among alternative lines of action can be made only in the light of clearly stated goals. Thus economic goals (such as growth, stability, efficiency, justice, security, and freedom) need to be identified clearly. They represent the value judgments of our society and of the people in it. Although economists operate within a framework of value judgments with respect to goals, they keep their prescriptions to a minimum.

Finally, to have economic understanding means the possession of certain skills, including the ability to interpret statistics and to use certain tools of analysis (economic theory), and a sense of the historical evolution of human events.

# 2

---

## *The Central Economic Problems in All Societies:*

### Wants, Scarce Resources, the Need for Decision Making, and the Need for an Economic System

"THE BASIC FACT which every economic system faces, some much more than others, is scarcity—the lack of enough productive resources to satisfy all the wants of its members. This basic fact of scarcity gives rise to the need for economizing—that is, for allocating the available productive resources so as best to satisfy the wants of the people . . . Since there are more competing wants than can be satisfied, some procedure is required for ranking or compromising the competing desires for what our scarce resources can produce." *Task Force Report,* p. 170.

### Economic Wants

Satisfying people's material wants for goods and services is the end purpose of economic activity. It is what economics is all about.

Economic wants are our wants for material goods (commodities) and services—things that are scarce in relation to the demand for them: food, clothing, automobiles, TV sets, pens, haircuts, medical attention, bus transportation, education, better housing, and national defense. They do not include such things as air, sunshine, ocean water, and sand at the beach because normally these are not scarce and they present no economic problem of production, exchange, or distribution. (See discussion of scarcity and economizing, pp. 170–172.)

We are not concerned in economics with such nonmaterial wants as the desire for friendship, a happy marriage, or religious satisfaction. (However, the cost of building a church or a jeweler's earning a living by selling wedding rings are economic aspects of these nonmaterial wants.)

Some of our wants are individual in nature—our own clothes, toothbrushes, or pencils—whereas others are collective. As families we have collective wants for the houses, cars, furniture, and TV sets we all use. As Americans we have collective or social wants for highways, post offices, and national defense from which we benefit as a people.

Some of our wants are for material goods such as clothing and cars; others are for the services performed by teachers, barbers, filling-station attendants, mailmen, soldiers, and congressmen.

Our economic wants are never-ending. Some are repetitive. We eat a meal but we get hungry again later. We have our hair cut but it grows again. We buy clothes but they wear out. Other wants appear as new things are invented and made available for the first time. Forty years ago we did not want television, antibiotics, ballpoint pens, jet planes, and nylon stockings because they did not exist. Furthermore, as the years go by the population increases, and there are more Americans in the country who have wants. Thus the economic wants of society are never satisfied.

## Consumption, Consumers, and Consumption Goods and Services

In economics the process of satisfying wants is called consumption and the people whose wants are satisfied are consumers. Consumption, or the use of goods and services to satisfy these wants directly, (e.g., eating food or burning coal) may take place quickly or it may take place over a long period of time (e.g., "consuming" a car by driving it for 10 years until it wears out or living in a house for 50 years).

Having a service performed (e.g., getting a haircut) is just as much "consumption" as wearing clothes or sitting in a chair.

Consumption goods and services are those that satisfy our wants directly (e.g., food) in contrast to capital goods (e.g., tools or machines), which do not satisfy our wants directly but help us produce what we want.

The typical unit of consumption in the United States is the household, which is a group of persons occupying a dwelling unit. Most households are families—that is, two or more persons related by blood, marriage, or adoption—although about one-sixth are persons living alone or in unrelated groups.

## Production and Producers

The goods and services that we need do not come to us without effort. They have to be produced. Food must be grown. Houses must be built. Teachers must be trained. TV sets and cars must be manufactured. Even earlier, farm tractors and fertilizer must be provided. Trees must be cut down for lumber, teachers colleges must be built, and iron ore must be mined and turned into steel.

The process of providing consumer goods and services as well as capital goods is called production and the people who carry on production are called producers.

People who perform services, such as barbers, insurance agents, truck drivers, and bank clerks, are producing just as much as people who are making something, such as the farmer growing food or the dressmaker sewing a dress. (Note: The middleman—so often attacked as unproductive—is actually productive because he is performing a service people want, such as insuring their goods, transporting them from one place to another, or wrapping them in cellophane.)

The typical unit of production in the United States is the firm, which, however, differs with respect to its legal form: individual proprietorship, partnership, or corporation. Varying greatly in size, it ranges from a giant like General Motors to a man running his own shoe-repair shop. Some production is carried on by government agencies: e.g., the post office or local fire department. Some production is carried on by the housewife who does household chores.

## Productive Resources or the Factors of Production

In order that our goods and services may be produced, certain basic means of production called the factors of production or productive resources are necessary.

There are three basic factors of production—land or natural resources, labor, and capital:

1. Land or natural resources, which are synonymous with the gifts of nature, include fertile soil, minerals in the ground, water and timber resources, and a climate appropriate for growing various crops. The ability of a society to produce is in part determined by the availability of natural resources. The United States and the Soviet Union have the advantage of being wealthy in natural resources, whereas Somalia and Jordan are not.

2. Labor is human effort; it includes the technical, managerial, and administrative skills of the people of a society. Both the number of

people and the quality of their labor are important. For example, Australia, like the United States in the eighteenth century, is short of people and could produce more if the population were larger. On the other hand, Indonesia has plenty of people but unfortunately not many of them are skilled and consequently it is not a productive nation.

3. Capital goods or capital are those means of production—like tools, machines, factories—that do not satisfy our wants directly but help us to produce what we want. In popular parlance capital is thought of as money, but if a businessman wants to raise "$5000 capital" it is to buy capital goods, raw materials, or labor services. So we draw a distinction between money capital and capital goods.

Sometimes a fourth factor of production is identified. The usual name is entrepreneurship, but reference is also made to the entrepreneurial function, which is the process of bringing the other three factors together and organizing production. Some aspects of this function can also be subsumed under "labor," since the entrepreneur is in part a special kind of worker, and some employees of large corporations, such as a general manager, perform many functions that might be considered entrepreneurial in nature.

## The Principles of Production

The Task Force Report emphasizes the importance of several aspects of the process of production (*Task Force Report,* pp. 174–177).

*Technological Progress*

In addition to the basic factors of production already identified, another important ingredient of production must be discussed. This is technology. Basically, the technology of a society is the way in which the industrial arts are applied. It embraces the instruments of production and the way in which production is organized. Thus an advanced technology, such as that of the United States today, includes both complicated machines and industrial processes (e.g., automated machines and petrochemical processes) and such aspects of industrial organization as mass production and the application of science to agriculture. The primitive technology still maintained in some underdeveloped countries depends on the use of primitive tools (the sickle and the digging stick) and the absence of scientific know-how.

9

*Division of Labor*

Division of labor, another term for specialization, takes several forms:

1. Individuals specializing in the jobs they are best fitted to perform by training, inherent skill, or efficiency resulting from practice; for example, in the home the family divides up the chores among its members and in the community teachers, doctors, filling-station attendants, and mailmen are persons who qualify for those particular occupations. Through specialization more work is done and more goods and services are produced than if everyone tried to do many different jobs.
2. Businesses specialize in producing certain products or services in, for example, automobile assembly plants, supermarkets, and canning factories. More can be produced this way than if, in addition to Chevrolets, General Motors tried to turn out frozen foods or if supermarkets tried to sell (and repair) automobiles as well as groceries.
3. Regions specialize in producing what they can do best; for example, Iowa grows corn, Idaho, potatoes, and Brazil, coffee, whereas Michigan builds automobiles, Sweden makes glassware, and Holland processes cheese. Trade, that is, exchanging what we produce for what someone else produces, enables everyone to enjoy this increased production. All modern economies, whether capitalist, communist, or socialist, are based on specialization and trade.

One consequence of specialization is that individuals, business, regions, and countries are now interdependent. All of us depend on others to provide many of the goods and services we want. This is true whether we think of ourselves as individuals, Philadelphians, Texans, or Americans.

*Labor Productivity*

The important point here is that real increases in production in a country like the United States are based to a large extent on the increased ability of each worker to produce, not on adding more workers as the population grows.

Each American worker has become more productive over the years (turns out more per hour of work) because he has acquired more skill and has been given better guidance and better tools and machines with which to work. Thus we have increased our production at a faster rate than our population and our living standards have gone up.

*Saving, Investment, and Capital Formation*

As discussed earlier, one of the key factors of production is capital—the plants, tools, and machinery that help us to produce the consumer goods we need.

Where does capital come from? Capital is the result of saving.

Leaving money out of the picture for the moment, saving and investing means not using productive resources to make consumer goods but to make capital goods instead. Saving thus means abstaining from consumption; for example, Robinson Crusoe saved when he took time off from catching fish (consumption good) to build a canoe (capital good). Building the canoe was capital formation. Our nation saves and invests when we use steel to make machines (capital goods) instead of refrigerators (consumer goods).

Now bring money into the picture, for in real life most saving is in the form of money. If we save money instead of spending it, we are not buying consumer goods. Instead we put our money in the bank or in other financial institutions (e.g., insurance companies), which can then lend our savings to businessmen so that they can buy or hire productive resources to build machines. When businessmen spend money on buying machines or constructing new factories, this is called investment. *(Note:* In economics the word investment has a special meaning—business spending on capital goods. Do not confuse it with the popular meaning of the word, which is *investing* in stocks and bonds or real estate.)

The productive resources that are not used when we save our money and refrain from buying consumer goods are now used to make capital goods for business. Thus real saving and money saving are closely related. The latter makes the former possible.

The more a country puts into capital formation, for instance, the more factories it builds, the more it can produce. Since capital formation requires saving, this means that consumers have to buy less now in order to have more later.

The Soviet Union is an example of a country that has put a large part of its productive resources into capital formation. As a result, its people have had to do without many consumer goods, but the economy has grown rapidly and they can hope to have more in the future.

It is important to realize that individual Americans are involved in this capital-formation process. They save their money and put it into financial institutions, which lend it to businessmen and home builders who then use it to buy or hire productive resources to make capital goods.

*The Principle of Diminishing Returns*

The principle of diminishing returns can best be understood by considering the case of a farmer who has a 300-acre farm. If he tried to cultivate all the land himself, he could produce a certain amount of wheat, but if he hired a farm worker to help him the two of them could perhaps produce more than twice as much (i.e., the application of an additional unit of one productive resource, labor, to a fixed amount of another, land, results in a more than proportionate increase in output). This would be increasing returns. If the farmer hired a second helper, perhaps the three of them could more than triple the original output, but he could not go on like that forever. If he could, then we would be able to produce all the food needed in the United States simply by adding more and more workers to just one farm. In reality, "diminishing returns" soon set in; that is, the added amount of food produced by each additional worker (what economists call the marginal product) would eventually start to fall off (after, say, the fifth man had been added) and eventually, when there were so many workers that they were getting in one another's way, the total amount produced would actually decrease.

Over a period of time, however, one way of staving off diminishing returns is by improvements in technology. In the United States more efficient farm machinery, new chemical fertilizers, and new pesticides have assisted in the production of more food with fewer workers. Our farm population is now falling but production is going up. Returning to the earlier point, labor productivity is rising. In India, however, where there is a shortage of farm machinery and fertilizer, this is not happening. As the population increases, more workers try to grow food on a fixed amount of land and diminishing returns are often a reality.

## Scarcity and the Need for Decision Making

The basic fact of economic life in all societies is that productive resources are scarce in relation to the never-ending wants of the people.

As individuals, we cannot have everything we want at once. Our incomes are limited and we have to make a choice between alternative ways of spending our supply of money.

As a society we cannot have everything we want at once. If we put productive resources into building rockets for national defense, we cannot put the same resources into the manufacture of cars. If we use land for a shopping center, we cannot also grow wheat or build a school on it. If we put resources into capital goods, we cannot use them to produce consumer goods. If a man is trained as an engineer, he cannot also be a doctor. Therefore we must make a choice with respect to the use of limited productive resources. Of course, if they are unemployed resources, they can be used to produce additional goods without reducing the output of others.

It should be noted here that the existence of unemployed resources in a society (e.g., unemployed people and idle factories during a depression) does not mean that everyone's wants have been satisfied and that there is no scarcity of resources in relation to the wants of the society. It simply means that a breakdown in social organization has occurred, with the result that the resources are not being fully utilized. The wants are still there.

The process of deciding how to use scarce resources when faced with alternative possibilities is known as economizing. It is also referred to as the allocation problem because we must decide how to allocate scarce resources among alternative ends.

One way of looking at the cost to a person or a society of satisfying a want is to consider the things foregone by not using scarce resources in an alternative way. The cost to the United States of national defense is all the houses, cars, hospitals, and schools we cannot have because we have to put so many productive resources into rockets and submarines. The cost to the consumer of buying a new suit is the weekend vacation he must give up to be able to afford the suit. The cost of capital goods, like machines, is the consumer goods that must be sacrificed by saving to buy the machines. This is known in economics as opportunity cost.

## The Need for an Economic System

Since all societies are faced with the same basic problem of economizing or allocating scarce resources to alternative uses, each society must have some organized way of dealing with it.

We use the term economic system to describe the organized way in

13

which the people of a society go about making decisions with respect to the use of their scarce resources.

Specifically, any economic system must provide answers to four questions:

1. What goods and services shall be produced? Since everything the society wants cannot be supplied, somehow a system of priorities must be established. What will be produced now and what will have to wait until later; for example, more capital goods now and thus fewer consumer goods or more national defense products and fewer civilian goods.

2. How shall goods and services be produced? Different possibilities exist for using the factors of production. Shall there be a large amount of labor and little capital (as in China, where highways are built by hand) or shall labor-saving machines be used as a substitute for labor (as in the United States, where automation is now taking over in many businesses)?

3. How much shall be produced in total? This means how fast shall the economy grow and how shall it obtain reasonably stable growth by avoiding both depression and inflation?

4. Who shall receive the goods and services produced? There has to be some way of deciding how what is produced shall be divided up among the people of the society.

Economic systems vary widely today and have done so throughout history. The central economic problem—the allocation of scarce resources among competing wants—has remained the same but the methods of dealing with it have varied widely.

Examples of economic systems in history are Pharaoh's Egypt, based on slavery and dedicated to the glorification of the ruler (pyramid building), the manorial system in medieval Europe, based on tradition, and the antebellum South, based on plantations, slavery, and foreign trade.

Examples of economic systems today are those that are loosely called capitalism, communism, and socialism, although these names are not very satisfactory, as we shall see later.

# 3

## The Modified Market Economy
## of the United States

"IN A BASICALLY PRIVATE enterprise economy, consumers' money demands largely determine what is produced. Businessmen, striving to make profits, try to produce those goods and services which consumers want. . . . The profit motive, operating under competitive pressures, largely determines how goods are produced. . . . Markets, in which prices rise and fall in response to relative demands and supplies, provide the links which mesh together the entire set of consumers and businessmen. . . . Thus, it is the demands of individual consumers, coupled with the desire of businessmen to maximize profits . . . and the desire of individuals to maximize their incomes . . . which together determine what will be produced and how resources are used to produce it." *Task Force Report,* pp. 174–175.

### Private-Enterprise Economy

A private-enterprise economy is one in which private citizens, either as individuals or grouped together as a corporation, partnership, or cooperative, are free to go into business themselves, produce whatever they estimate consumers will want to buy, and make a profit if they are right in their estimate or suffer a loss if they are wrong.

A private-enterprise economy is different from a communist economy in which the government makes the decisions about what to produce.

A private-enterprise economy also means that private persons may own productive resources (private property). They may hire labor, gain control over natural resources, own capital goods, and use them to produce goods and services for sale at a profit. The concept of private property in the United States embraces not only the ownership of productive resources but also certain rights, including the right to determine the price of a product or to make a free contract with another person.

15

Because government in the United States has come to play a significant economic role and because private enterprise now has to operate within a framework of many government controls, our economy is often referred to as one of modified private enterprise or even a mixed economy, that is, a mixture of private and government decision making.

An example is the railroad industry. Railroads in the United States are privately owned and try to make a profit by providing the public with transportation services. Nevertheless they operate within a framework of strict government regulations with respect to the fares and rates they can charge and the type of service they can offer. Their property rights have been limited over the years, although this limitation has been based on "due process of law."

Most private enterprise in the United States is not subject to such strict government controls as the railroads, but all are under some regulations that restrict their freedom of action; for example, they cannot indulge in misleading advertising. For this reason the term "free enterprise"—often used to describe the American economy—is not so accurate as private enterprise or modified private enterprise. In addition, the existence of monopoly in some markets means that free enterprise in its pure form does not truly exist in the United States.

### Profits and the Profit Motive

Profit, loosely defined, is the difference between receipts and costs—what a business has left over after subtracting the cost of producing goods and services from the amount received from selling them to its customers. It is the reward of the producer for organizing and carrying out production.

The possibility of making a profit is the incentive that encourages producers to produce. This is the profit motive.

The profit motive is not only the incentive to engage in private enterprise but also to produce particular goods and services and to shift from one line of production to another in response to shifts in consumer demands. An example of the profit motive at work was seen when it became apparent some years ago that the American consumer wanted small rather than big cars. After noting the increase in sales of small European cars, American producers were led by the profit motive into producing compacts.

When producers are persuaded by the profit motive to shift from old to new lines of production, they move productive resources from one use into another. Thus we see how the decisions of individual producers, directed by the profit motive, constitute part of the mechanism for deciding what will be produced in the United States.

The other part of the market mechanism is, of course, the freely made decisions of consumers in regard to spending their money and what they want to buy. The changing pattern of consumer desires and the responses of producers to this pattern are the two key elements in a private-enterprise economy in determining the allocation of resources and what will be produced.

Some modern economists are concerned with the extent to which large businesses, by intensive advertising, are able to influence consumer wants and, at least in the short run, control the pattern of demand instead of responding to consumer decisions.

## The Circular Flow of Income

"The model [of the circular flow of income] is still an oversimplification of the modern American economy. It can, however, provide a useful framework for analyzing and evaluating the functioning of such an economy—a broad picture of the entire economic system. . . . They [such models] do not pretend to describe the real situation except in broad outline. They provide guides for thinking about particular situations or problems—not answers to them. They are tools of objective, rational analysis of how the economic system performs." *Task Force Report,* p. 167.

The circular flow of income in general is the picture we would get of our whole economy if we were able to remove ourselves from participation in it and look at it from a distance as one can look at the ant world in one of those glass-fronted ant hills sold in variety stores.

As an individual ant, we should have little conception of the total pattern of activity in the ant hill, yet this pattern is clear to the human observer who can see the whole. A chart of the circular flow of income is a model that reveals the over-all pattern of activity in our own economy.

The main circular flow of income involves business and the public:

1. Business hires or buys productive resources (labor, capital, and natural resources) from the public and pays them wages, salaries, interest, and rent in return.
2. The wages, salaries, interest, and rent received by the public

provide them with income, which, as consumers, they spend on the goods and services produced by business with the productive resources acquired.

3. Thus there is a circular flow of money payments—from business to the public in the form of income and from the public back to business as money spent on goods and services.

4. This circular flow of money payments is matched by a flow in the opposite direction of productive resources and finished goods and services. Productive resources flow from the public to business (e.g., workers provide their labor) in return for which the public receives income in the form of wages, and so on. Business uses the productive resources to produce goods and services which then flow back to the public (in return for which business receives money income spent by the public).

A second circular flow of income involves the public and the government:

1. The public pays taxes to federal, state, and local governments and in return receives public services from such sources as the post office, highways, and schools.

2. Government uses the tax money to hire or to buy productive resources from the public.

3. Thus there is a circular flow of income from the public to government in the form of taxes and from government back to consumers in the form of wages, salaries, interest, and rent.

4. This circular flow of money payments is matched by a flow in the opposite direction of productive resources and finished goods and services. Productive resources flow from the public to government (in return for which the public receives money income). Government uses the productive resources to produce goods and services (e.g., schools and highways), which then flow back to the public (in return for which the government receives income in the form of taxes paid by the public).

The third circular flow of income involves people in their capacity as savers and investors:

1. People do not dispose of all income by spending and paying taxes. They normally save part of it.

2. These savings are put into financial institutions, which lend them to business.

3. Business uses the money it borrows (together with the earnings it saves itself) to acquire productive resources from the public by paying them money income. These resources are used to make capital goods. Thus productive resources are drawn away from the production of consumer goods and services but are paralleled by a reduction in consumer spending as a result of the saving.

The significance of the circular flow of income is that it provides us with a simple framework or model for understanding the functioning of the whole economy. It is a simplified model, of course, but other elements of the real world, such as the role of banks, which can expand the flow of spending by creating money, as in loans to customers, can be introduced as desired. Many important economic problems (e.g., inflation and depression) are explained today in terms of changes in the flow of spending. Thus the concept of the circular flow of income is a useful tool of analysis.

### Markets

The market is the basic institution of the American economy. For this reason we talk of the "market economy," the allocation of resources "by the market," and leaving or not leaving economic decisions "to the market."

Basically the American economy is one of decentralized decision making. The answer to the question who decides what goods and services will be produced and who will get them is: "We all do—all of us in our capacity as consumers, producers, workers, savers, and investors when we make free decisions in the market, based on our tastes and desires and on the amount of money we have if we are consumers and workers and on our aspirations for profit if we are producers." To the extent that large businesses, large unions, or the government are able to dominate particular markets, decision making ceases to be decentralized and is concentrated in the hands of those who have economic power. In the United States today considerable economic power is concentrated in the hands of big business, big unions, and big government.

The market is the mechanism that permits us to register our individual economic decisions. A consumer who has decided to buy a Volkswagen rather than a Buick, a college graduate with a major in physics who has decided to go into industry rather than teaching, a manufacturer who has decided to produce color rather than black-and-white TV sets—all are making decisions "in the market."

Originally, a market was actually the place (e.g., the village square) at which buyers and sellers came into physical contact. Although such places still exist (e.g., a farmer's roadside stand), in modern America the market is now better described as an organized situation that permits buyers and sellers to deal with one another. Because of modern methods of communication (e.g., the use of the telephone) and modern marketing methods (buying by sample or description from intermediaries such as wholesalers), buyers and sellers no longer have to be in physical touch with one another.

The market adds up the individual decisions of buyers and sellers and converts them into aggregate forces known as demand and supply. It is this demand and this supply, interacting with each other, that determine the price of a good or service, and it is prices that serve as the principal regulators of economic activity in a private-enterprise economy.

In modern America, for a variety of reasons (moral, social, and political), we do not permit all goods and services to be provided by private enterprise in the system of markets. Education, national defense, highways, and police and fire protection are just a few examples of the areas in which we have substituted direct government action for the impersonal market mechanism.

## Demand and Supply

*Demand*

An individual's demand for a product is indicated by a table that shows the different amounts he would buy at different prices at a particular time. Other things being equal, the lower the price is, the greater the quantity demanded, and the higher the price is, the lower the quantity demanded.

The total demand for a product is indicated by a table that shows the total quantity demanded by all individuals at each of the different prices.

We should distinguish between the "demand schedule" in the sense of a table of different quantities that will be bought at different prices and "the quantity demanded" or the quantity that will be bought at a particular price. A change in price will change the quantity that will be bought but it will not change the demand schedule.

Demand is not the same as want. Demand means want backed up

by an ability and willingness to pay the price prevailing in the market. A student who wants a Cadillac convertible or a mink coat has no economic significance in terms of the functioning of the market unless he or she has the money to buy these items and is willing to spend it.

The quantity of a product that will be demanded at a given price will depend on the following:

1. Consumer tastes and preferences which can be influenced by advertising.
2. The availability of alternative or competing products.
3. The amount of money that consumers are willing and able to spend.
4. The prices of other products that will serve the same purpose.

A change in any of these factors is likely to bring about a change in the demand schedule—that is, in the amounts that will be bought at different prices.

*Supply*

The total supply of a product is indicated by a table that shows the total quantity to be offered for sale in the market by all producers at each of the different prices. Other things being equal, the higher the price is, the more offered for sale, and the lower the price, the less offered for sale. In the United States today, because of the growth of big business, the supply of a good may come from only a few producers; for example, there are only four automobile producers in the country. At the other extreme, however, cotton is supplied by thousands of individual farmers.

In the long run the quantity of a product that will be offered for sale will depend largely on the cost of producing it in relation to the price at which it can be sold. This takes us back to our definition of profit and to the fact that profit acts as a stimulus to production.

*Elasticity of Demand*

The concept of elasticity of demand refers to the extent to which the quantity demanded will increase if the price is lowered by a given amount or decrease if the price is raised.

EXAMPLE: The demand for salt is inelastic for the quantity demanded does not change much following a change in price. We would not buy and eat more salt just because it was cheaper. Generally speaking, the demand for necessities tends to be inelastic. The demand for  color TV sets, however, is elastic. If the price comes down, more people will buy them. Generally speaking, the demand for luxuries tends to be elastic; that is, the quantity demanded changes quite a bit after a change in price. If fur coats went up in price by 50 percent, many women would stop buying them. When good substitutes exist, price elasticity tends to be high; when few substitutes exist, it tends to be low.

One practical example of this concept is in the field of taxation. A tax on a product raises its price to the consumer. Therefore the government finds it advantageous to tax products, such as gasoline and cigarettes, that people regard as necessities and for which there are no satisfactory substitutes because the higher prices will not greatly reduce the quantities that will be sold. Since people go on buying the products, the government will collect the tax revenue it wants. A tax on a product with an elastic demand would tend to defeat itself by reducing the volume of sales and thus lessening the government's tax revenue.

## Prices

The price of any commodity is its exchange value in terms of money.

In a competitive market prices are determined by the interaction of the forces indicated by demand and supply schedules. Prices are a reflection of the combined decisions of individual consumers to buy and of individual producers to sell.

Although price is the usual term for the monetary value of goods exchanged in the market, sometimes other terms are used with reference to services; for example, the price of labor is called a wage or salary, the price of an apartment is rent, and the price of borrowed money is interest.

Changes in prices are the main regulators of economic activity in the United States. In fact, it is often said that we have a price-directed economy. As a general rule, if prices are raised, sales will decrease and the quantities offered for sale will rise; if prices fall, sales will increase and the quantities offered for sale will decrease. Thus a change in prices tends to bring the two quantities in line; for example, if only 1000 units of a particular product are bought in one week at 5 dollars but 1200 are offered for sale at that price, the price tends to fall until, say, at $4.75 the quantities taken and offered balance at a figure less than 1200.

Specifically, price changes reflect changes in the scarcity or abundance of a commodity in relation to the demand for it and thus constitute a rationing system that decides which consumers will get the product and which will go without; in other words, it decides who gets what is produced.

If a commodity becomes scarcer, its price will be bid up, some consumers will be unwilling or unable to pay the higher price, and the goods will go to those who can.

If a commodity becomes more abundant, its price will go down and more consumers will be able to buy it.

Price changes also indicate to producers what is profitable or unprofitable to produce.

If consumers want more of a product, they will bid its price up, thus making it more profitable to produce it and indicating that production should be increased. Producers will then increase their demand for productive resources, taking them away from commodities that are in less demand by consumers. Producers of goods that are less in demand will suffer losses and may even go out of business. These "penalties" will persuade them to shift to the production of something else that they hope consumers will buy.

Finally, prices indicate how something should be produced; for example, a comparison of the price of a computer and of the wages of 10 clerks might persuade a business to use more capital (computers) and less labor (clerks) in production.

Thus prices determined in markets by our decisions are the ultimate sources of the patterns of production and consumption. In other words, it is the people of the United States who decide how our productive resources will be used and what goods and services will be produced.

It should be remembered that the foregoing analysis shows what happens in competitive markets. If a market ceases to be competitive because of the appearance of monopolistic factors, the price mechanism will not necessarily work in the way described (see p. 182).

## Competition

An essential part of the market mechanism in a price-directed economy is competition, which can be defined as economic rivalry among sellers for the customers' dollars or among producers as they seek to buy the factors of production.

The characteristics of a competitive market are the following:

1. A large number of buyers and sellers, though there may be competition of a certain kind even when there are only a few sellers.

2. Reasonably complete information among the buyers (and sellers) regarding the nature of the product, its availability, and the availability of alternatives.
3. Reasonably free entry into the market for new sellers who may be attracted by the profits being made.

*Price Competition*

Traditionally, competition has been thought of in terms of price competition; that is, getting business away from a competitor by lowering prices. Competition among sellers for the consumer's dollar, if fully operative, forces the price of the product down to the lowest level consistent with covering costs of production, including a reasonable or necessary profit.

*Nonprice Competition*

Competition today also takes other forms, such as improving a product by adding something a competitor lacks (e.g., putting power steering on a car), improving the way in which it is sold (wrapping vegetables in cellophane), or by vigorous advertising to persuade the customer that a product is better. This is known as nonprice competition and it can occur even when there are only a few sellers (e.g., automobile producers).

*Effects*

Competition among sellers tends to promote efficiency and to put pressure on producers to improve the quality of their products, to develop new products, or to reduce their prices to attract customers away from other sellers. Thus competition (a) guarantees consumers the product they want at relatively low prices and (b) leads producers into using scarce productive resources in the most efficient way. To sum up, competition tends to produce a similarity of interest between the producers who wish to make profits and the consumers who want the maximum amount of high quality goods at minimum prices. Under competitive conditions the producers who give the most satisfaction will usually make the most profit.

Competition, in addition to benefiting consumers, provides opportunities to people to set themselves up as producers to share in the profits being made by those already in business. Thus competition is part of our private-enterprise system, which emphasizes opportunity and profit for the producer and benefit for the consumer. These results do not accrue unless competition is actually present.

Some forms of nonprice competition, for example, excessive advertising, may actually raise the cost of the product and therefore be harmful to the consumer.

## Monopoly

"Where monopoly exists to an appreciable degree (in the markets for goods or for labor), society cannot rely on the market to bring about the most effective allocation of resources in response to consumer demands. . . . The problem of enforcing reasonable competition is thus a complex and difficult one." *Task Force Report,* p. 182.

In reality the American economy is not one of "pure" competition and completely free private enterprise. All economic decisions are not made in free competitive markets under the impersonal forces of demand and supply. This is partly because government often intervenes in the market and partly because of the existence of monopoly.

Monopoly is said to exist in a market when there is only one seller (e.g., the telephone company) or when there are only a few sellers who work to avoid most of the elements of effective competition among themselves, perhaps by agreeing on a price higher than that which would prevail if there were real competition or by dividing up the market and staying outside one another's territory.

The main economic significance of monopoly is that it makes it possible for a producer to increase his profit by selling a smaller quantity of his product to consumers at a higher price. Thus consumers are denied the benefits of competition. The result is that productive resources are no longer allocated in response to consumer demands; moreover, they are no longer allocated to satisfy the most wants.

The rise of the monopoly problem has come about largely as a result of the rise of big business over the last 100 years.

When a market no longer contains a large number of sellers but only a few big ones, history shows that monopolistic behavior becomes possible; for example, there are relatively few producers of steel, electrical equipment, tires, plate glass, aluminum, air brakes, and metal containers today. In 1961 several big electrical equipment manufacturers were convicted in a federal court of conspiring to fix prices.

The rise of big business, however, has come about mainly as a result of the evident advantages of low-cost mass production. Without mass production, which requires big business, we would not enjoy our present high living standards.

## Public Policy Toward Monopoly

There have been two public policy responses to the problem of monopoly. One has been the passage of the antitrust laws, beginning with the Sherman Act of 1890. The other has been the growth of direct government regulation of business, beginning at the federal level with the Interstate Commerce Act of 1887.

The basic philosophy of the antitrust laws is that competition is good and monopoly bad and that the federal government should therefore enforce competition by breaking up monopolistic businesses, such as the Standard Oil trust in 1911, or by prosecuting businesses that reduce competition by agreeing on prices, as in the case of the electrical equipment manufacturers in 1961.

One of the dilemmas facing the enforcers of the antitrust laws is that it would be a mistake to assume that all big businesses are bad and should be broken up. How we can enjoy all the advantages of big business (mass production, and research and development needed to provide new products) and still protect ourselves against the abuses of power that bigness makes possible is the issue facing us.

The other response to the monopoly problem has taken the form of government regulation of business. Most of the regulated industries are known as public utilities.

Examples at the federal level are the Interstate Commerce Commission's regulation of the railroads; at the state level, the state public utility commission's regulation of electric power companies; and, at the local level, regulation of city transit companies by the city authorities.

Government control in the main takes the form of fixing the price or prices charged by a business and regulating the quality of the service or services provided. The government regulatory authorities try to fix a price that will be fair to the consumer, yet will also enable the business to earn a reasonable profit.

The economic significance of public-utility regulation rests in our recognition that the impersonal market mechanism cannot work to our satisfaction in certain areas and therefore we seek to substitute government decision making for the decisions of the free market.

The main characteristics of regulated industries are the following:

1. They are usually vitally important to the public; for example, electric power producers.
2. Competition would be wasteful (e.g., it would be foolish to tear up the street to lay down two competing water mains), and therefore it seems desirable to have a "natural monopoly but one that must be regulated in the public interest.

## Economic Role of Government

"It is important for students to understand that, even in a basically free enterprise economy, governments play a significant role in setting priorities and using resources—that is, in deciding what to produce and how to produce it." *Task Force Report,* p. 185.

The American economy is one of modified private enterprise. It is a "mixed economy," for although the majority of economic decisions are made by buyers and sellers in the market, significant ones are also made by the federal, state, and local governments. Thus government plays an important role in deciding how productive resources will be used.

One important economic function is regulatory. Federal, state, and local governments regulate a wide range of economic activity by limiting the freedom of action of individuals and businesses. The purpose of this regulation is to promote the general welfare, to protect certain groups, or to see that certain things are done in the interests of justice that might not be done if they were left to the market.

EXAMPLES: To protect depositors the federal government regulates banks through the Federal Reserve System and insures bank deposits through the Federal Deposit Insurance Corporation. It also protects certain manufacturers by imposing a tariff on foreign imports that compete with similar products made in this country. State governments regulate the establishment of businesses with state corporation laws and enforce the maintenance of certain health standards in restaurants. Local governments enforce building codes and zoning laws.

By regulating the activities of private persons and businesses government influences the way in which productive resources are used.

The most significant activity of government today is its direct influencing of the allocation of resources through its taxing and spending.

When government imposes taxes on citizens or businesses, it takes money away from them and thus transfers control over productive resources from them to itself.

EXAMPLE: If a man pays 1000 dollars in taxes, his ability to buy such things as cars and clothes is reduced by 1000 dollars, but the government's ability to buy such things as rockets and planes or to build highways is increased by that amount.

When government spends money to purchase goods and services in the market (public expenditures), it is bidding resources away from private use. It is gaining control over a quantity of resources that is no longer available to private citizens because they have paid their taxes and thereby lost that much capacity to acquire resources for their own use.

These taxing and spending operations of the government constitute an income flow to and from what is called the public sector of the economy in contrast to the private sector of the economy in which private consumers and producers operate in the market.

How many of our productive resources will be diverted from the private sector to the public sector by the process of government taxing and spending is decided in the United States by the political processes of free elections and congressional and state legislative action. Congress votes tax laws that set tax rates (e.g., the tax reduction measure of 1964) and votes the appropriations for such programs as national defense, foreign aid, and the "war on poverty."

In addition to buying goods and services from private producers, the government is, of course, a producer itself. Federal, state, and local governments are in business to provide postal service, operate schools and public libraries, produce electric power in government-owned facilities such as Grand Coulee, and run municipal bus lines, to mention a few.

The importance of the public sector can be gaged by the fact that in recent years government has purchased more than 20 percent of the nation's total production and employed about 12 percent of the labor force.

The economic issues that are considered in deciding whether goods and services should be provided by the public or private sector include the following:

1. Can an essential service be provided at all by the private sector? Obviously, national defense cannot and therefore it is controlled by the public sector.

2. Can a service, if handled by the private sector on a profit basis, be made available to as many people as we wish to receive the service? Education can be provided by the private sector and is to a considerable extent in private schools, but if everyone is to go to school, regardless of his ability to pay, we must have public schools and finance them by taxation.

In addition, the government makes what are called transfer payments to many private persons. These are payments for which no goods or services are received in exchange, such as unemployment compensation, veterans benefits, welfare payments and farm subsidies. When government taxes certain people and "transfers" the money in this way, it is affecting the distribution of income and thus influencing the shares of what is produced that citizens will receive.

The extent to which the government should increase or decrease its economic participation must be considered by citizens in the light of such goals as freedom, efficiency, security, justice, stability, and growth.

## Other Market Imperfections

Another modification of the free market mechanism occurs when those who must make decisions in the market have less than perfect knowledge of the alternatives facing them. Consumers, for example, may not be well informed or may be strongly influenced by the producer's advertising. Workers may not know of job opportunities. Small businessmen may not be aware of the extent of the competition they face or of the volume of demand for their products. In such cases the market mechanism will not function as smoothly as it should. Other imperfections are racial discrimination, which may hold down the mobility of labor in certain markets, and the tendency of many consumers to buy on impulse or because of a prevailing fad. The economic case for such public policies as truth-in-packaging laws to protect the consumer, civil-rights legislation to break down barriers to employment, and the provision of information on market conditions to small businesses by the United States Department of Commerce is that these measures permit the market mechanism to function more efficiently.

# 4

## Economic Growth and Stability

"STUDENTS need to be introduced to the fact that many of our greatest economic problems center around how to obtain stable economic growth, avoiding the excesses of the inflationary booms and depressions. . . . Economic stability and growth of total output are among our most important objectives. They are broad goals on which virtually everyone agrees. . . ." *Task Force Report,* p. 191.

Economic growth and stability, the broad goals on which virtually everyone agrees, were formally established as national objectives by the Employment Act of 1946, which requires the federal government "to promote maximum employment, production, and purchasing power."

### Economic Growth

Economic growth means increasing the national output of goods and services in the nation over a period of years at a faster rate than the population is increasing so that there will be more for each person. In this way living standards can rise. The term used is increase in per capita output.

In the United States per capita output has risen spectacularly over the years and has established our living standards at their present high levels. This has not always happened, however, in some of the under-developed countries of the world in which the population is increasing rapidly and production only slowly. An example is India.

Rapid growth is important so that we can raise our living standards (not only our private living standards but our public ones as well; that is, so that we can have not only more cars and TV sets but also more schools and hospitals) and so that we can provide enough jobs as the population grows and the labor force becomes larger. The labor force of the United States will have grown from 82 million (in 1970) to 90 million by 1975, and the extra people seeking jobs will be able to find them only if an expanding economy provides them.

The upper limit to growth is set by the nation's productive capacity, which depends on the quantity and quality of productive resources available and on the level of technology.

Production requires the mobilization and utilization of the factors of production. The ability to increase production is dependent on the ability of the society to accomplish the following:

1. An increase in the number of workers—either by normal population growth, as in the United States since the 1920s, or by immigration, as in the Common Market or Australia today.
2. An increase in the quality of the labor force by making workers more productive through formal education or on-the-job training.
3. An increase in its stock of capital goods so that it will have more machines, tools, and factories to produce goods and services. This requires that more of the nation's resources be saved and channeled into investment and fewer into consumption goods. One of the objectives of the 1964 tax reduction legislation in the United States, which lowered taxes on corporate profits as well as on personal incomes, was to encourage investment and thus spur growth.
4. Improve its technology and managerial competence by carrying out research, inventing new machines, and discovering better ways to organize production. Automation is an example of advancing technology.

In a private-enterprise economy, in which goods and services are produced only if it is profitable to do so, an increase in effective demand is also a prerequisite of growth. Effective demand means actual spending by consumers, business, government, and foreigners on goods and services.

If all of these groups together spend enough to take off the market at profitable prices all the goods and services the economy is currently producing, the incentive will be to increase production, and growth will take place within the limits set by the availability of the productive resources.

If, however, effective demand is not large enough, some productive resources will be thrown into idleness (unemployment, closed factories), and not only will there be no stimulus to increase output but there will be actual pressure to decrease it.

Thus economic growth in the United States requires both an expansion of the nation's physical capacity to produce and an increase in effective demand (total buying or spending) for goods and services.

31

The level of effective demand is in part a function of real factors, such as population growth, and in part a function of monetary factors; that is, whether the money supply of the country is allowed or caused to expand so that people will have enough to increase their spending. The latter point has come up frequently in American history. One occasion was during Jackson's fight with the Second Bank of the United States, another during the "free silver" controversy after the Civil War and during William Jennings Bryan's campaigns for the presidency, and still another during the Great Depression of the 1930's. More recently an inadequate growth of effective demand is thought to have been the principal cause of the slow growth of the period 1957–1962, a state of affairs the tax cut of 1964 was designed to remedy.

## Economic Stability

Economic stability means keeping the economy on an even keel as it proceeds along the road of growth, avoiding the twin evils of inflation and depression.

Inflation occurs when the price level rises noticeably. This means a reduction in the purchasing power of each dollar in the hands of the consumer, which hurts particularly those whose incomes are fixed and those who are living on pensions and annuities or who have accumulated savings. During the years 1946–1948, and again during the Korean War and the war in Vietnam, sharply rising prices created hardships for many.

Depression or recession occurs when productive resources are substantially less than fully employed. It means unemployment, falling production, declining profits for business and "hard times" in general. The difference between a depression and a recession is merely one of intensity and scope. The Great Depression of the 1930's lasted 10 years and was characterized by widespread unemployment and tens of thousands of business failures. The recession of 1960–1961, a much milder affair, lasted less than a year and did not affect some people or some businesses at all.

### The Problem

If the economy is likened to an automobile on a highway (the road of growth), we want it to proceed at an adequate and steady speed toward its objective. This is the rate of growth. We also want it to stay in the middle of the road and not slide off into one of the roadside ditches.

One ditch is inflation. The other is depression. Sliding into either, in addition to being painful in itself, can interrupt progress along the road of growth.

Stability is thus the nation's immediate short-run objective, whereas growth is its long-run goal.

## Measuring the Performance of the Economy

The proper use of statistics is at the basis of economic decision making. We cannot tell how well or how poorly our economy is doing with respect to its goals, nor can we formulate the correct policies to deal with our problems unless we have specific statistical information.

A prudent family operates on a household budget and keeps a record of income and expenses. This enables it to make wise decisions with respect to the use of its scarce money resources by budgeting for current expenses, vacations, college educations, and medical expenses.

A business keeps records of its financial transactions. The record of its assets and liabilities (and net worth) is called the balance sheet and the record of its income and expenditures is called the income statement. The system of financial records is known in its simplest form as bookkeeping and in its more sophisticated form as accounting. These records provide businessmen with the specific information they require to make decisions regarding production, investment, and sales.

Similarly, during the last 35 years economists and statisticians have developed a system of statistical records for the American economy as a whole—what all of us together produce, spend, consume, save, and invest. This is known as social or national income accounting.

These statistics tell us how well the economy is performing—how fast it is growing or whether we are moving into a depression or inflation—and provide the basis for public policy decisions—whether to lower or raise taxes or to encourage business investment in other ways; for example, the 1964 tax cut was designed to stimulate economic growth and the 1968 tax increase, to curb inflation, but these decisions had to be made on the basis of specific information, not generalities.

One of the two most important statistical concepts used in social accounting is the Gross National Product (GNP). The GNP is the dollar value of all the goods and services produced in the United States in one year. In 1968, for example, the GNP was 866 billion dollars, which was the total value of all goods and services turned out by our economy during the year.

The GNP can be broken down initially into four subdivisions based on the buyers of goods and services. Thus the GNP figure reflects total spending as well as production. The four buyers of the GNP are consumers who buy consumer goods and services, business which buys capital goods, and government and foreigners who buy both (e.g., local government hires teachers, state government builds highways, and federal government buys pens for use in post offices).

The GNP is of basic importance because it gives us a reasonably accurate picture of how much altogether we are producing and, over a period of years, how fast or slowly our total output is growing; this is the rate of growth. In the short run changes in the GNP also show us whether we are declining into a depression or expanding into prosperity.

The GNP is measured in dollars, and each good or service is valued at its final market price. Therefore we must be careful not to let a rise in prices give us a generally false picture of the growth of the economy; for example, the GNP in 1929 was 104 billion dollars, but in 1970 it is expected to be 990 billion or more than nine times as much as 41 years ago. This does not mean that we are actually producing eight times as many goods and services because the price level (the average of prices) has doubled during this period. A pound of butter was 35 cents in 1929; now it is about 80 cents. A wool suit that cost 30 dollars in 1929 now costs 80 dollars. A textbook that cost 2 dollars in 1929 now costs about 8 dollars. So statisticians have developed a measurement of real GNP or real output, which eliminates the price changes and measures GNP in different years at one constant level of prices. The figures that result are a better basis for comparing the economy's performance over the years.

The second of the two most important statistical concepts in social accounting is the National Income. This is the total of all the income we earn for producing goods and services—all the wages and salaries earned by workers for contributing their labor to production, all the interest and rent received by those who lend money or land to producers, and all the profits made by producers as a reward for their efforts in organizing production.

The National Income can be subdivided in many ways; for example, a breakdown will show how much is earned in each state or in each of the main sectors of our economy, such as industry and agriculture. Above all, these figures give us a picture of the various sources of income and their uses. They tell us what people and businesses do with their incomes—how much they pay in taxes, how much they spend, how much they save, and how much of the profits of corporations are paid out as dividends and how much is reinvested.

Two other related statistical concepts should be mentioned. One is personal income, which is the total income received by individuals from all sources during the year. It is the total of wages, salaries, pensions, dividends, transfers, and other forms of individual income but excludes income received by corporations. The other is disposable income, which is the amount a person has left after he has paid taxes to the government. There are only two ways of disposing of disposable income: it is spent or saved. Thus disposable income is equal to the sum of consumer spending as it appears in the GNP and personal savings. The figures on disposable income give us a partial picture of the amount of purchasing power in the hands of the American people. It does not give us a complete picture, however, because consumers can draw on accumulated savings and borrow if they want to spend more than their disposable incomes.

Other statistical devices for measuring economic performance are known as index numbers, which are percentage figures used to measure such things as the cost of living and industrial production; for example, the cost of living (the average of prices paid by consumers for such typical things as food, clothing, and medical care) in 1957–1959 is regarded as a starting point and made equal to 100. If these prices on an average rise 30 percent, as had happened by 1970, the index for the current year becomes 130. Government figures are issued every month so that we can determine whether there is inflation and to what degree.

## Main Forces Determining the Level of National Production and Income

One question of fundamental importance is: What determines whether we will have economic stability in the short run? What are the factors that produce inflation, depression, or recession? Why is there sometimes prosperity, in which employment, income (national income), and output (GNP) rise, and at other times recession or even depression, marked by increasing unemployment and falling income and output?

The simplest answer is that total spending or total effective demand varies considerably in the short run. If total spending by consumers, business, government, and foreigners increases faster than the quantity of goods and services we are actually producing, the economy acts like an auction mart and prices go up as too many dollars chase too few goods. This is inflation.

If total spending is too low and the goods and services produced cannot be sold, business profits will be reduced and businessmen will be forced to cut back on production and lay off workers. This in turn (remember the circular flow of income defined earlier) will reduce the flow of spending still further and the effects thus spiral downward.

The least predictable element in total spending which has moved up and down the most in recent years, thus causing expansions and contractions in the economy, is private investment; that is, business spending on tools, machines, and new factories. This has been so for several reasons:

1. One is the psychology of businessmen who make investments with future profits in mind. Their expectations with respect to profits may be optimistic or pessimistic (e.g., the 1964 tax cut made many of them optimistic) and this affects the volume of investments made.

2. After a certain period of building new plants and buying new machinery the time comes when industry is well supplied with such things and needs to digest them. They have increased their productive capacity and now a time must elapse to allow consumer demand to catch up with what they can produce with the added facilities. For a time investment falls off, only to increase later when the capital equipment begins to wear out and needs replacing and when increasing consumer demand requires a further expansion of productive capacity.

3. New products and advances in technology occur irregularly and cause changes in investment spending; for example, in United States history such developments as the railroad boom, the invention of the automobile, the development of electricity, and the introduction of the Bessemer process in the steel industry all caused "bursts" of investment spending.

4. Business spending on inventories, that is, on stocks of goods held in warehouses, storerooms, and showrooms, varies considerably, depending on sales to consumers and on businessmen's expectations. From the end of World War II until 1948 businessmen bought goods from manufacturers not only to resell to consumers but also to stock up their showrooms, which had been emptied during the war. By 1948 inventories had been built up to satisfactory levels and business

spending on them decreased. Thus, even though consumers went on buying, the demand for goods produced by manufacturers fell off and we had the "inventory recession" of 1948–1949.

Variations in business spending result in changes in consumer income, since consumers in the circular flow of income are on the receiving end of the payments made by business. When incomes fall, consumer spending may fall too, thus further reducing the profitability of business and again setting in motion the downward spiral.

Depression and inflation feed on themselves. There is a snowball effect in which changes in business and consumer spending, production, and income reinforce one another. This relationship has been called one of dynamic interdependence. The technical terms used to describe this are the "multiplier" and the "acceleration principle."

### Fiscal Policy for Economic Stability

"We now realize much better than we did a few decades ago that government budget policy can play an important stabilizing role in a potentially unstable economy." *Task Force Report,* p. 194.

When we have analyzed the nature of the problem of economic stability, measured its scope, and determined as best we can its causes, we can move on to a consideration of how to deal with it. As already mentioned, the responsibility for taking action was imposed on the government by the Employment Act of 1946.

Two major public policies are available to us for promoting economic stability. One is fiscal policy, the other, monetary policy. Both are concerned with influencing effective demand either upward or downward, depending on whether the problem is depression or inflation.

Fiscal policy is the policy of the federal government with respect to taxing, spending, and managing the national debt.

Government spending is an important part of total spending, for government purchases of goods and services at present constitute about 20 percent of the GNP. In addition, the government sometimes pays out more than it receives in social security collections. These, and certain other payments, like veterans pensions and interest on the national debt, are called transfer payments, as already noted. If the federal government builds a post office or buys uniforms or food for the armed forces or a local government buys books for a public library, they are counted in the national income accounts as government purchases of goods and services. The government is acquiring productive resources and paying for them with money payments to business and households. If the government pays unemployment compensation to an unemployed worker or a pension to a disabled veteran, however, it is not acquiring productive resources but merely making a transfer payment to him out of current tax collections.

The important point is that government, by its spending, whether on purchases of goods and services or by transfer payments, is maintaining or increasing total spending and thus maintaining or increasing income and employment. If the government reduces its spending, the reduction acts as a depressant on income and employment.

When the government raises taxes, as it did during World War II, the Korean War, and in 1968, it takes money away from consumers and business and this reduces spending in the private sector. If taxes are cut, as in 1964, more income is left in the hands of consumers and business, which permits an increase in total spending.

*Compensatory Fiscal Policy*

A comparison of the totals in federal government spending and taxing for one year, as is done in the federal budget, will result in a budget surplus if tax receipts exceed expenditures or a budget deficit if expenditures exceed receipts.

The significance of this is that a budget surplus reduces total spending because government is taking more from consumers and business in taxes than it is paying out to them by spending, whereas a budget deficit stimulates the economy because government is putting more money in the hands of consumers and business by its spending than it is taking away from them by tax collections.

Variations in government taxing and spending, as revealed by the federal budget, constitute the heart of modern fiscal policy. It is by these changes that the government tries to bring greater economic stability to the economy. The idea is to boost total spending to check a recession caused by low demand and to curb it to fight inflation caused by excessive demand. The government seeks to act as a sort of balance wheel, often called compensatory fiscal policy because it is trying to compensate for fluctuations in total private spending.

*National Debt*

One important fiscal policy issue is the debt of the federal government.

The national debt increases when the federal government fails to collect enough in taxes to cover its current spending and therefore has to borrow. *(Note:* The public debt includes the debts of state and local governments as well as the national debt of the federal government; that is, it includes such things as school bond issues.)

The federal government borrows by selling government securities to banks, insurance companies, pension funds, and any other institution or person willing to lend money to the government. These securities include the familiar Series E Savings Bonds, which are purchasable only by individuals.

The important thing to remember about the national debt is that its size should be related to national income and production. A dime is a big debt to a second-grader who is getting an allowance of 25 cents a week (it is 40 percent of his income) but not to an adult getting 100 dollars a week (then it is 1/10 of 1 percent of his income). Similarly, though our national debt today is large, it has not grown so fast as the income and production of the nation since World War II. At the end of World War II the national debt was 275 billion dollars and the GNP was 214 billion. Today, although the national debt has grown to over 360 billion, the GNP has passed the 930 billion mark. Also, because there are more people in the United States today (204 million compared with 140 million in 1945), per capita national debt has actually decreased.

The existence of a substantial national debt has other implications, but the National Task Force did not feel that the details must be understood by high school students except in broad outline. They should, however, at least know that the government has to pay interest on the money it borrows and that this interest now amounts to about 16 billion dollars a year, or 8 percent of total federal spending.

### Money, Banking, and Monetary Policy for Economic Stability

"Although students should be introduced to money and banking, it is too much to hope that they can master all of the intricacies about them which are found in college textbooks. Emphasis should be put on comprehending a few basic relationships and on an elementary understanding of how the chief monetary institutions operate." *Task Force Report,* p. 195.

High school graduates should have three major areas of understanding when it comes to money and banking.

1. What is money and what is its function in our economy?
2. Where does money come from?
3. How does the government try to control the money supply and for what purposes?

*The Nature and Functions of Money*

Students should know that the most important kind of money in the United States is not coins and not bills but checking accounts, bank accounts, or deposit currency, as it is variously called. The technical name for this kind of money is demand deposits, so called because the depositor can get his money from the bank on demand. The depositor spends this kind of money by writing checks, which are simply his instructions to the bank to transfer amounts in his checking account to other persons. This is done by means of bookkeeping entries by the bank.

Three obvious functions of money are to serve as a medium of exchange, as a measure of value, and as a store of value:

1. Money serves as a medium of exchange because it is acceptable to all of us and therefore eliminates the need for barter. The barber who wants his shoes repaired does not have to find a shoe repairman who wants his hair cut. All of us will readily accept money in return for goods or services we are willing to supply because we know others will accept it in turn from us.
2. Money serves as a measure of value because it enables us to measure economic activity just as tons and pounds enable us to measure weight and just as miles and inches enable us to measure distance. An example of this function is that we say a gallon of gasoline costs 30 cents, the GNP is 930 billion dollars, or our weekly paycheck is 100 dollars.
3. As a store of value, money provides us with an easy way of saving. It is easier to save by depositing money in our bank accounts than to store canned goods, clothes, furniture, and automobiles in our basements for future use.

In the broader context of the functioning of our economy our whole system of specialized production and of buying and selling goods in markets requires the use of money. Since economic growth and economic stability are closely related to the level of total money spending by consumers, business, and government, obviously the amount of money available to Americans is important. It is not only the quantity of money available to us that is important but also the rate, called the velocity of circulation of money, at which we spend it. One dollar can change hands many times in a day and finance many transactions. If people spend money more rapidly or more slowly than before, more or fewer business transactions can be financed with the same quantity of money.

Where does money come from? The *Task Force Report* says: "Bank deposits, against which checks can be written, result chiefly from the lending and investing activities of banks."

This means that consumers borrow money from banks to buy a car, businessmen to buy new materials or tools, would-be homeowners to buy a house, farmers to buy a tractor, and so on. The federal government borrows from the banks when it does not collect enough taxes to cover its expenditures. If the bank agrees to lend the money, it opens a checking account against which the borrower can write checks.

Thus the banks create most of the money we use by lending to consumers, businessmen and other borrowers, and by buying the bonds that the government offers for sale. Every time a bank makes a loan or buys bonds it is creating a demand deposit or checking-account money. Similarly, when a loan is repaid by the borrower, demand deposits are wiped out. This process is often called creating credit, meaning credit money. At the same time the borrower is going into debt. Thus the creation of money can be thought of as banks creating credit money or as people, businesses, and the government going into debt by borrowing from banks.

The creation of money in this way is limited. First, a borrower must be a good risk; he must put up some sort of security for the loan and pay interest. Second, the government, through the Federal Reserve System, puts a limit on the amount of checking-account money the banks can create. This limit is set by requiring the banks to have reserves, which must be not less than a certain percentage of their demand deposits. Thus the size of the reserves determines the ability of the banks to lend. Since reserves need be only on a fraction of total deposits, our money supply is said to be based on a fractional reserve system. These reserves, for most banks, take the form of deposits that each member

41

bank must have at the Federal Reserve Bank in its district.

How does the government try to control the money supply and for what purposes? Here we are concerned with what the *Task Force Report* calls "the close tie between reserves, which provides the monetary authorities with the means to control the lending and deposit-creating activities of the banks." The basic points here are the following:

1. The principal control mechanism of the government is the Federal Reserve System which consists of the Board of Governors in Washington and 12 Federal Reserve Banks around the country.
2. The name given to the process of controlling the lending and deposit-creating activities of the banks is monetary policy or monetary management. A good definition of monetary policy is that it is the government's policy with respect to the supply of bank-credit money.
3. The purpose of monetary policy is to promote economic growth in the long run and economic stability in the short run.

Remember that growth and stability are largely a function of total money spending and that monetary policy is an important way of influencing it.

If a recession threatens, monetary policy makes it easier and cheaper through lower interest rates for people to borrow money and thus increase their spending, or total demand, for goods and services. If inflation threatens, monetary policy makes it harder and more expensive at higher interest rates to borrow money and thus reduces spending and the total demand for goods and services.

In the long run monetary policy seeks to allow total spending to increase enough to finance economic growth. If there is to be long-run growth in production, there must also be long-run growth in the amount of money so that the extra goods and services may be purchased without a drop in the price level.

The techniques used by the Federal Reserve authorities to bring about an expansion or contraction of the money supply, and thus of total spending, are complex, and the *Task Force Report* states that students need to understand them only in a general way:

1. The thrust of monetary management is that most of the reserves, except the cash, of the member banks, the size of which determines how much money they can create by lending, must be held with the district Federal Reserve Bank.

2. The Federal Reserve authorities can do certain technical things that will either increase or decrease the size of these reserves and thus affect the money-creating ability of the banks.

*The Effectiveness of Monetary Policy*

The *Task Force Report* urges (p. 197) that students be taught that there is disagreement among experts on the effectiveness of monetary policy. In this connection the following points are relevant:

1. Although there is a connection between the amount of money created by the banks and the total spending of consumers and business, it is not a rigid one; for example, spending can increase without a rise in the money supply if people spend money at a faster rate. An example of such an increase in the velocity of the circulation of money came during the first few weeks of the Korean War when people wanted to stock up on nylons and automobile tires, which they thought would soon be in short supply and more expensive, before the hoarders got them. Monetary policy could do little about it.

2. Similarly, just making it easier for banks to lend does not necessarily mean that people will actually borrow the money that is available, especially if they lack confidence in the future. This happened during the Great Depression of the 1930's, when total spending did not increase as much as was hoped in spite of the Federal Reserve's policy of making it easier for banks to lend. Businessmen were not too eager to borrow because of the poor outlook for profits and the prevalence of other economic uncertainties; and consumers who wanted to borrow money to meet their current household needs while unemployed were not good credit risks. Thus the banks, even with ample capacity to lend, did not make many loans.

3. It is important to remember too that changes in spending can, as the *Task Force Report* says (p. 196) "lead to either increases in output and employment or to a rise in prices or to both at the same time." This means that if productive resources are lying idle, as during a depression, an increase in total spending will mean a greater demand for goods and thus for the workers to make them. In such a situation the output of goods and the employment of workers will rise as the idle resources are put to work. This was the idea behind the great increase in government spending on public works during the

Great Depression of the 1930's. It also means, however, that if total spending increases when there are no idle productive resources to be put to work, because they are already fully employed, as in wartime, prices will rise as buyers compete for scarce goods.

As the *Task Force Report* says (p. 198), the conclusion is that "monetary policy can have a substantial effect on spending—and thus on output, employment, and prices," but it is not a precise never-failing instrument of policy with guaranteed results.

### The Role of Gold

Two important points must be remembered with respect to the role of gold:

1. The laws that once required that a certain amount of gold be held as a backing for our money supply have been repealed. There is now no relation between the amount of gold held by the government and our domestic money supply. Moreover, Americans are not permitted to possess gold except for nonmonetary purposes, such as dental fillings.

2. Gold is still the ultimate means of settling debts between countries. Countries have different monetary systems and use different names for their monetary units. We operate with dollars, the French with francs, and the Spanish with pesetas, but gold is universally accepted. Therefore, if Americans make payments to foreigners (buying their goods, lending them money, or giving them foreign aid) which in total are greater than the payments they make to us (for buying our goods, repaying loans, or using our ships and planes), at least part of the difference will be settled by transfer of ownership by the Federal Reserve System of some of our gold to other countries. This has been happening on a substantial scale in recent years.

If we lost too much gold, we might not have enough to meet still further transfers abroad. Students should consider here whether we would change the rules if this situation developed. Consider the significance of the old saying: "Money will not manage itself."

### Cost-Push and Administered Price Inflation

The first paragraph on p. 199 of the *Task Force Report* points to what is called cost-push inflation. This is the problem we face when an upward push of costs (especially wage costs) rather than increased consumer demand is the factor behind a rise in prices.

This factor is often encountered in markets in which prices are not determined by the impersonal forces of demand and supply but are administered by the heads of big business and unions that dominate the market. Thus the term "administered prices" is often used and sometimes occasions government action. The steel industry offers a good example. The wages of steelworkers (the price of their labor) are determined by a group of union and company officials who negotiate a contract between the union and industry. Thus wages are not set by the market but by agreement. Similarly the price of steel can often be arbitrarily raised and maintained by the big companies, although even then only within limits. Students may read about President Kennedy's famous controversy with the steel industry in 1962 as well as the 1968 efforts of President Johnson to roll back steel prices.

If wages and prices rise as a result of this process, which can happen even when there is unemployment and the steel mills are not in full operation, monetary and fiscal policies are not the answer. The problem is not one of excessive total spending but rather of the concentration of economic power in the hands of big unions and big business.

# 5

## The Distribution of Income

"The third big economic question which all economic systems must answer is: who shall receive the goods and services the economy produces and in what proportions?" *Task Force Report,* p. 202.

### Market Determination of Income

The main point made by the *Task Force Report* on page 203 is that the market in general determines how much income, in terms of money, people will receive and their money income determines the share of the goods and services they can have. The value of the goods and services people can buy with money income constitutes real income.

Students should refer back to the concept of the circular flow of income in which people receive money income (wages, salaries, interest, rent, and profits) for contributing their productive services. The actual amount each will receive is determined in the market for his particular service. For example, in the different income groups there are relatively few brain surgeons and a great demand for their services; hence their "price" (income) is high, but the demand for unskilled workers is low and there are many of them; hence their "price" (income) is low. In addition, of course, many persons receive transfer payments from the government.

### Economic Justice

In addition to describing how it is decided who will get what, the *Task Force Report* raises the question of economic justice (p. 202) by asking, "are incomes distributed too unequally . . .?"

When it asks if taxes should fall more heavily on upper income groups, it refers to the fact already noted that government taxing and spending can bring about a redistribution of income by taxing more heavily the people with high incomes and spending it on public housing, public education, public-health facilities, and other federal programs which benefit the people with lower incomes. Thus the government can—and does—redistribute income.

The *Task Force Report* also has in mind that private groups, such as labor unions, can influence the distribution of income by using their economic power in the market in collective bargaining processes to raise wages above what they would be if left to the free market.

The pursuit of economic justice may be defined as the application of our concepts of what is right and what is wrong—of what ought to be— to economic policy. Over the years the nation has concerned itself increasingly with those whose share of our national output has been considered inadequate. Programs to provide the needy with better housing, education, and job-training facilities and the elderly with medical and hospital care are examples of this policy.

## Role of Profits

The *Task Force Report* says (p. 203) that profits in the general or business sense "represent a combination of payments for managerial services, entrepreneurial risk-taking and the use of capital." Economists often use the term in a much narrower sense to include only the net gains after all allowances for wages of management and interest on capital have been made.

This means that business profits are in part a reward for the very special kind of labor performed by the entrepreneur who runs a business—for example, the storekeeper who runs his own store—in part a reward for taking a chance on a new product or a new business, and in part simply the return that investors get for allowing their savings to be used.

This analysis underlines the fact that profits are important in a private-enterprise economy not only as income to business but also as an incentive to produce.

A worker receives his wages as payment for his labor, but he is working on a contractual basis for an agreed-on hourly, weekly, or monthly income. Profits, on the other hand, are a surplus that may or may not exist after all contractual costs have been deducted from total income.

This element of risk taking, together with the incentive or possibility of profit involved, is a key feature of our economy.

## Personal Distribution of Income

When the *Task Force Report* refers to the gradual reduction of inequality in income distribution and gives the reason for it (p. 204), it is once again referring to the ability of the government to redistribute income by taxing and spending and to the ability of certain organizations, such as unions, to influence this redistribution.

The reference to poverty in the United States (*Task Force Report*, p. 204) again places emphasis on the functioning of the market. Market conditions change (e.g., we now use less coal but more oil and also fewer unskilled workers and more machines because of automation), and the demand for certain types of labor changes accordingly (e.g., we need fewer coal miners and more computer operators). Requirements of skill, racial discrimination and lack of knowledge of job opportunities, prevent the people who are no longer needed in one occupation or in one part of the country from moving into new jobs elsewhere. Thus people become unemployed and join the ranks of the low-income or no-income earners.

An important cause of the present poverty problem in the United States is that many workers lack the education and skill needed to perform the jobs being created by the new technology. Others in the poverty classification are many old people, members of minority groups, marginal farmers, and broken families headed by women.

## Labor, Wages, and Labor Unions

The key point here concerns labor productivity. In the final analysis what workers can earn will depend on their productivity—that is, their output of goods and services. If more is produced, the business can sell more and there will be more money to pay the workers higher wages.

Real wages—that is, the amount of goods and services a worker can get with his money wages—have gone up over the years because productivity has gone up. Statisticians try to measure productivity by comparing inputs of labor (man-hours of work) with output of goods. For example, if the number of pairs of shoes produced with an input of 10 man-hours of work (10 workers working one hour) goes up from 100 to 103, there has been a 3 percent increase in productivity.

Increases in productivity occur partly as a result of giving workers more effective tools and machines to work with, partly from an improvement in their knowledge or manual dexterity based on education or experience, and partly because of the more efficient organization of their work processes.

Increasing productivity and the consequent increase in the GNP are thus attributable to the workers themselves, the investors who make capital available, and improvements in managerial skills. For example, in the automobile industry, workers now have greater skills, all sorts of automatic equipment such as the turret lathe, and a management that has improved its knowledge over the years through experience and formal education.

## Unions and Collective Bargaining

To understand the role of unions we must remember that there is a labor market in which the workers, who constitute the supply of labor, try to get the highest prices for their services while the employers, who constitute the demand for labor, are trying to get those services at the lowest prices. The formation of unions and the development of collective bargaining in which the unions represent all the workers instead of each worker bargaining individually has given workers more power and enabled them to obtain higher wages and better working conditions, sometimes at the expense of management. Unions have thus affected the distribution of income.

Two further issues are raised by the *Task Force Report* (p. 206) in connection with unions.

1. Featherbedding by unions, like protective tariffs and monopolistic restrictions on output by business, provide an opportunity to apply "the central proposition that high wages and other incomes depend basically on high real output." Featherbedding occurs when a union forces an industry to hire more workers than it needs, as happened years ago when the railroads agreed to put firemen on diesel locomotives. Protective measures can benefit a particular group at the expense of others but they do not increase total production. Indeed they involve a misuse of productive resources for the benefit of the few and at the expense of others. For example, a tariff keeps an industry going which could not otherwise survive the competition of foreign producers. Thus it keeps scarce productive resources employed in a relatively inefficient way when the economy as a whole would benefit from their transference elsewhere. A specific example would be allocating United States resources to the watch and pottery industries, thus preventing their use in the more efficient industries that produce business machines and construction machinery.

2. The other issue raised is that "economic groups obtain their income

objectives partly through the political processes as well as through the market place."

This is a reference to the fact that many business, labor, and farm groups are able to influence Congress or their state legislatures to pass legislation beneficial to them in terms of larger incomes. Examples are farm price supports, minimum wage laws, fair-trade laws (under which the merchants in some states can escape the price competition of discount stores), tariffs, and oil depletion allowances, under which oil companies may deduct as much as 22 percent of their gross income before calculating their taxes. This compensates for the depletion of an irreplaceable natural resource.

## Farm Incomes

"The 'farm problem' should be understood broadly by students." *Task Force Report,* p. 207.

The important thing to remember about the farm problem is that it should be examined in the light of economic concepts already learned.

*Growth*

Agriculture is an excellent example of increasing productivity brought about by an advancing technology and the use of capital. As a result, output per acre and output per man-hour have risen, and we are producing more and more in spite of the fact that the number of farm workers diminishes year by year. This growth of farm output has actually created a problem, since the supply of many agricultural products has tended to outstrip the demand for them at any price high enough to cover the cost of production. The demand for many basic crops, such as wheat and cotton, has tended to grow rather slowly. People do not eat much more bread, for example, when their incomes rise, and synthetics, such as nylon, have cut into the demand for cotton. Rapidly increasing supply and lagging demand have contributed to the creation of surpluses that greatly depress prices.

*Stability*

The farmer has always been particularly vulnerable to depression when the price of wheat drops sharply but his debts and the prices of what he buys remain stable. Traditionally farmers have not been averse to a little inflation, since it means that the burden of their debts is lightened. The historic support of farmers for "free silver," the Populist movement, and the New Deal programs are evidence of this. It was the depression-created havoc in agriculture in the 1930's that persuaded the government to launch its program of price supports for farm products.

## The Market Mechanism

In a free market many small farmers are unable to earn a satisfactory income because the persistent tendency of supply to outstrip demand has a depressing effect on prices. For this reason we have had government price supports for many years. The question to be considered here is the relative merits of two different methods of allocating agricultural resources—the free market and government controls like price supports and production controls.

## The Desire for Economic Stability

The issues posed by the section of the *Task Force Report* on economic security (pp. 207–208) include the following:

### Economic Justice

To what extent should society take care of its less fortunate members; for example, the unemployed and the sick? Medicare is one current aspect.

### Economic Stability

To what extent do payments to the unemployed, for example, provide spending power to help support the economy and keep a depression from deepening?

### Economic Efficiency

Do private pension plans reduce the mobility of labor and thus lessen the efficient use of resources? Is it a serious matter that a New York educator some years ago changed his mind about accepting a job as head of the California State College System because he would have to give up his lucrative New York pension rights?

### The Compatibility of Economic Goals

Is there a conflict between the desire for security and the risk-taking that is part of the growth process?

# 6

## The United States and the World Economy

### Importance of World Trade and Investments
### to the United States

"The United States is increasingly tied to the rest of the world, in economic as well as political matters." *Task Force Report,* p. 187.

This "tie" exists because of the importance of exports, imports, and international investment.

The United States exports about 35 billion dollars of goods each year, and the incomes of many farmers, the jobs of many workers, and the profits of many businesses are dependent on the sale of those goods in foreign countries, particularly agricultural and mass-produced and sophisticated industrial products. For example, the United States normally exports one-third to one-half of its wheat and cotton crops, 40 percent of its civilian aircraft, and 25 percent of its construction machinery. A company like Gillette (shaving supplies and beauty aids) earns as much as 30 percent of its income from overseas markets.

Imports are necessary for the growth of our economy. Some products, like tin, nickel, and coffee, we do not produce. Other products, like copper, bauxite, petroleum, and iron ore, we do not produce in adequate quantities to take care of our GNP and population growth. For example, our domestic sources of iron ore, the Minnesota mines, are now inadequate.

International investment is important to the United States, for American businesses abroad help to produce what we need—for example, oil from Venezuela, which is obtained as a result of American investment of capital and know-how, which the Venezuelans lack. American capital abroad also helps to develop other countries into better markets for our exports. For example, Canada's 20 million people are our best customers because they have high incomes, but their incomes are high partly because American businesses have invested captial to advance production and thereby create well-paying jobs.

## Basis of World Trade

World trade takes place for the same economic reasons that trade occurs within the United States—because it pays to specialize in what you can do best and to buy from others what they can produce more cheaply than you can.

This is the basis for trade in wheat and oranges between North Dakota and Florida; it is also the basis for trade in automobiles and coffee between the United States and Colombia.

What an area can produce efficiently depends on the quality and the availability of productive resources, which are distributed unevenly around the world. Specifically, climate, soil, the presence of minerals, the supply of skilled labor and managerial talent, and the availability of capital differ from region to region. Compare the Pacific Northwest and the South, the United States and Mexico.

What is called the theory of comparative advantage is important here. Because productive resources are relatively scarce, it will pay a region to use them to produce those goods and services in which its advantage over other regions is great, thus leaving the other regions to produce those goods and services in which their advantage is slight. Students can understand this principle by asking themselves whether a top business executive who can also type would spend three hours of his working day typing his own mail or whether he would have a secretary to do it for him, even though she could not type quite so fast. What economists call "opportunity cost" is involved here (see p. 13). The opportunity cost of using resources in ways where your advantage over others is less pronounced is their diversion from uses where your advantage is more pronounced. Thus specialization on the basis of comparative advantage increases total output of goods and services.

Although the economic reasons for trade between nations are the same as for trade between different parts of the same country, special problems arising from the existence of political boundaries and independent governments distinguish international from domestic trade. Among these problems are different monetary systems and artificial trade barriers such as tariffs, neither of which exist within a country like the United States.

## Economic Problems in World Trade

Special problems in world trade are present because each country has its own money, its own central bank, and its own monetary policy.

*Foreign Exchange Rates*

If you want to trade with another country, you have to change your money into that of the other country. This is done in the foreign exchange market. The price you pay for the foreign money is the rate of exchange; for example, 92.5 cents in United States money for one Canadian dollar and 8 cents for one Mexican peso. It is the foreign exchange market and the various policies followed by different governments in that market that constitute the "elaborate financial mechanism" referred to on p. 188 of the *Task Force Report.*

Although, basically, demand and supply conditions interact to determine the exchange rates, most governments, including that of the United States, intervene in the market to keep these rates steady at an agreed-on level. The focal point of international monetary cooperation today is an institution called the International Monetary Fund, which now has a membership of over 110 countries.

*Balance of Payments*

The balance of payments is a statistical record of all the transactions that the people, businesses, and government of a country have with the rest of the world. It includes both receipts from the rest of the world (such as the proceeds of export sales or the income from foreign investments) and payments to the rest of the world (such as for purchases of imports, the provision of foreign aid, and investments abroad by private business). The study of a nation's balance of payments reveals, among other things, the items that are important in its international transactions; for example, tourism for Mexico and Switzerland, income from foreign investments for Britain, and foreign aid for the United States.

The balance of payments also shows how a deficit, which is an excess of payments over receipts, is covered. For example, the balance of payments of the United States in recent years shows why we have been losing gold and going into debt to other countries.

The existence of a deficit in the balance of payments also explains why many countries, for instance, India, have to maintain exchange control. Exchange control is a system under which anyone wanting to obtain foreign money must first have his government's permission and anyone receiving foreign money must surrender it to his government, which then rations it out to those who want it. Exchange control thus permits a government to ration scarce foreign money according to a system of priorities, with preference going to people who want to import a commodity, such as machinery, that will help the country's development.

Note that exchange control means that the free market is not allowed to work in the field of foreign exchange. Here again direct government controls are substituted for the impersonal forces of demand and supply.

## Tariffs

Since free trade is accepted as desirable inside a country, why do all nations impose obstacles to the free movement of goods between countries by imposing tariffs, which are taxes levied on foreign goods? There are several reasons:

1. The protection of new industries that are just getting started. Alexander Hamilton used this argument in his *Report on Manufacturers* in 1791 when he advocated protection of the "infant industries" of the United States against those already established in Britain, which had experienced the Industrial Revolution and had greatly lowered their costs of production. Today Mexico, Canada, and other countries use the same argument against the United States. The important point here is that these countries are putting economic growth, or the development of new industries as the objective of national policy, ahead of getting goods as cheaply as possible to the consumer now.

2. The provision of economic self-sufficiency in time of war. The watch industry of the United States used this argument to get a higher tariff by declaring that it needed protection from Swiss competition so that American watchmakers would be available as precision-instrument workers in time of war. Here again it is a question of goals. This argument places national defense ahead of benefit to the consumer as the goal for which to strive. Consumers in the United States pay more for watches in peacetime because of the import tax on lower priced Swiss watches in order that an important resource (watchmakers' skills) may be available in wartime.

3. The protection of jobs and wages of domestic workers against the competition of the lower wages of foreign labor. This argument has often been used in the United States against Japanese goods. Remember, however, that a product cannot necessarily be sold at a lower price just because its employers pay lower wages than their com-

petitors. Labor is not the only productive resource used in production. Even though wages in the United States may be higher than those in Japan, we may have other advantages, such as an abundance of capital, which make our workers much more productive and enable us to produce and sell many goods more cheaply.

EXAMPLES. California rice can undersell Asian rice in parts of Asia in spite of the great wage difference in Asia's favor. This is because Asian rice is planted and harvested by hand, while California rice is planted and harvested by machines.

The United States sells plastic toys to Japan because our petro-chemical industry is technologically more advanced than that of Japan.

West Virginia coal undersells British coal in Britain because our mines are mechanized and the seams of coal are more accessible, whereas British mines still use much hand labor.

In each of the above examples the American worker is paid higher wages than the foreigner. It is productivity that counts, not just the wage rate alone.

Tariffs may benefit individual industries or parts of a country but at the expense of consumers, who usually pay more, and of national efficiency in resource use. Tariffs perpetuate less efficient industries and the use of scarce productive resources that would be better employed elsewhere. Nevertheless, they might possibly be justified under certain circumstances as a price worth paying to achieve other objectives, such as growth or national defense.

# 7

## Other Economic Systems

"EVERY INFORMED AMERICAN should have a general impression of how other types of economic systems operate, especially communism. . . . Different economic systems solve the major economic questions (what and how, how much, and for whom) in different ways." *Task Force Report,* p. 209.

### The Spectrum of Economic Systems

The starting point for an understanding of other economic systems is the fact that all societies face the same central economic problem: how to use scarce resources (what and how to produce, how much, and for whom). But throughout history different societies have approached the central economic problem in different ways. This point was made more fully in Chapter 2.

The important thing today is that some economies, like the United States, rely primarily on the market mechanism, with a restricted role for the government, to find answers to the central economic problem, whereas others rely heavily on centralized decision making.

Centralized decision making may be comprehensive and autocratic, as in the Soviet Union, or limited and democratic, as in Britain and India. In Britain, for example, the Labor Party, which won the elections in 1945, quickly put more emphasis on central planning and introduced government ownership of productive resources (e.g., the coal mines and the steel industry). When that party was defeated in 1951 and the Conservatives returned to power, many of the policies were reversed and greater reliance was placed on the market. In 1964 another election brought the Labor Party back with a renewed emphasis on government controls and economic planning.

Most countries today are "mixed economies" in that some decisions are made in the market and others by a central authority, either democratically or autocratically. The important thing is the nature of the mix.

Even in the Soviet Union there is a limited free market for some agricultural products.

It is particularly important to avoid classifying economic systems into three rigid and unchanging categories called capitalism, communism, and socialism. The differences in the world of communism between such countries as the Soviet Union and Yugoslavia are now significant, as are the differences between the economies of the democratic West; for example, between the United States and France or between Switzerland and New Zealand. Finally, most of the underdeveloped countries are in their formative years with respect to their economic institutions. We are not sure how they will turn out.

## The Changing Nature of Economic Systems

All economic systems change over the years, even that of the Soviet Union. In the United States in the last 100 years we have seen such changes in our economic system as the rise of big business, the rise of labor unions, and a growing economic role for government. In the Soviet Union we have seen the growing importance of income differences as an incentive to production. Britain became less socialistic during the 1950's, whereas Egypt became more so. Yugoslavia has retreated somewhat from communism during recent years, whereas Cuba has moved toward it.

The study of economic systems should emphasize the different approaches to the central economic problem and the changes in these approaches over the years. It should also emphasize the performance of different economic systems in the light of such criteria as growth, stability, efficiency, security, justice, and freedom.

# PART TWO

# GRADE PLACEMENT OF ECONOMIC CONCEPTS

*James D. Calderwood*
*John D. Lawrence*
*John E. Maher*

TEACHERS and other curriculum developers are aware that any model curriculum that encompasses what every high school graduate should understand cannot be realized by every student. Thus in curriculum there is a need to economize and choices must be made. This is necessary even for those academically able students who achieve all of their learning in a school system that offers a continuous developmental program from kindergarten through high school.

The seven areas of economic understanding identified in Part One provide a convenient framework for relating economics to the social-studies curriculum. Only from this standpoint do they represent minimal citizenship requirements. Collectively, the seven areas are greater than the sum of the parts, but only if students are able to understand interrelationships. Moreover, students can develop a fairly sophisticated degree of economic reasoning without having touched all areas of application in the discipline.

From the standpoint of curriculum we should expect students to extend their grasp of whatever is economic about human behavior. In this sense economics, like other disciplines, is a vantage point for viewing behavioral phenomena. To develop this economic perspective a student at his own level of development must have adequate opportunities to observe human affairs and ask the questions that an economist might raise.* Of course, some behavior will contain little that is readily understood through economic analysis, but surprisingly often, economic implications can be found in the everyday conduct of human affairs.

## The Central Economic Problem

The following sequence of ideas which confronts all societies adds up to what economists call the central economic problem and constitutes the jumping off point for an understanding of economics.

WANTS. Economics is the study of man's means of satisfying his wants for goods and services.

CONSUMERS AND CONSUMPTION. When man satisfies his wants, he is a consumer. The end purpose of much economic activity is consumption.

*For a discussion of economics as *perspective* contrasted with *applications,* see John E. Maher, *What is Economics?,* John Wiley & Sons, New York, 1969, especially Chapter 4, "What Economics Is," and Chapter 5, "What Economics Is Not."

PRODUCERS AND PRODUCTION. The goods and services man wants must be produced. The process of creating the goods and services to satisfy these wants is called production.

PRODUCTIVE RESOURCES. Production requires the use of productive resources—natural and human—and capital goods.

SCARCITY. Productive resources are scarce in relation to man's wants for goods and services and are capable of alternative uses.

THE NEED FOR DECISION MAKING. The relative scarcity of productive resources and the fact that they are capable of alternative uses requires every society to make decisions. Specifically, every society has ways of deciding what goods and services will be produced with its scarce productive resources, how they will be produced and in what quantities, and for whom; that is, how they will be divided among the people of the society. Finding answers to these basic questions, *what, how, how much,* and *for whom* is known as the allocation problem.

THE NEED FOR AN ECONOMIC SYSTEM. Every society needs an organized approach to decision making—a set of procedures and institutional arrangements that will permit decisions to be made. We call these arrangements the economic system of the society. The central economic problem never changes but economic systems have varied throughout history.

## The Main Characteristics of the American Economy Today

High school graduates should be familiar with the main characteristics of the particular economic system now operating in the United States. This means understanding that the United States has a modified market economy in which most economic decisions are made in the market, by all of us, in our capacities as consumers, producers, workers, savers, and investors. Important economic decisions are also made by the people collectively through government and in some cases by private groups, such as big business and big unions, which have attained positions of power. Key concepts of this modified market economy include markets and prices, competition and monopoly, private enterprise, the profit motive, and the economic role of government. Other concepts cover households, banks, and labor unions.

It is particulary important to understand that the American economy is constantly changing and to know what these changes are.

62

## The Performance of the American Economy

High school graduates should have had some experience in evaluating the performance of the American economy in the light of certain criteria, among which are growth, stability, efficiency, security, justice, and freedom. Such an evaluation will lead the student to some appreciation of the various governmental policies designed to resolve problems and to improve the performance of the economy. These matters include monetary, fiscal, and antitrust policies and social security and antipoverty programs.

The performance of the American economy, judged by orthodox interpretations, has been generally excellent. Nevertheless, there is increasing concern about the undesirable consequences of economic activity. Students should learn that the results of productive activity include not only goods and services but "bads" and "disservices" such as air and water pollution, urban poverty and congestion, and a military-industrial complex that President Eisenhower warned could threaten our nation's security and freedom. Besides, a system that gives so much time and energy to the rapid creation of wants for goods and services raises doubts that it can satisfy them.

## The World Economy

Since the United States is deeply involved in the world economy, high school graduates should become familiar with certain international economic relationships and the ideas underlying them. These include:

· *Why international trade takes place*
· *The arguments for and against protectionism*
· *The significance of international investment*
· *The basic principles of international monetary relations*

A familiarity with international economic relationships and ideas will help students to understand the economic problems of the underdeveloped countries, the European Common Market, and the place of gold in the balance of payments.

## Basic Principles

Before discussing the introduction of these basic economic understandings into the curriculum, it will be useful to identify certain basic principles that should be kept in mind.

1. Economics is a social science and should be introduced in a planned way into social-studies courses at all levels, kindergarten through

the twelfth grade. There are many opportunities for integrating economics with other disciplines. In the lower elementary grades, for example, learning about the home and the community provides opportunities for relating the economic concept of specialization to the other, more familiar things already taught. In higher grades economic topics like the tariff can be discussed as political and economic issues; racial discrimination can be discussed from sociological, political, and economic viewpoints. There are numerous other situations, particularly in junior and senior high, in which an economic topic can be discussed within the exclusive framework of economics as a discipline; for example, the model of a competitive market or the theory of comparative advantage in international trade with two countries and two commodities.

2. The introduction of economics into the curriculum should be a developmental process. The knowledge acquired in each grade should lead to what is to be learned in the next, and the economic content of each grade should be regarded as part of a planned comprehensive approach to economics in the curriculum in which economic topics are related to one another and appropriately placed in the over-all context of the whole.

3. This subject is only a part of social studies and the objective is not to change elementary social studies or courses in American history or civics into an economics course. Nor is it sought to put economics into every classroom topic. On the contrary, the goal is to enrich what is already being taught with economic themes.

4. Students at all grade levels should extend their economic perspectives by viewing increasingly complex situations. It is the economic perspective that is crucial, not the multiplicity of applications.

5. The techniques used to introduce economics into a course must be appropriate to the particular teacher as well as to the student.

## Economic Concepts in the Primary Grades

Teachers in the primary grades can help pupils to develop certain basic economic ideas and concepts that will build a foundation for a more sophisticated appreciation of economics at a later age and that can easily be introduced by the usual *home-community* method used by early elementary teachers.

In the primary grades emphasis should be on the sequence of related ideas that add up to the central economic problem.

## Economic Concepts in the Upper Elementary Grades

In the upper elementary grades there should be further emphasis on the basic ideas and concepts that make up the central economic problem but at a more sophisticated level. At this stage the learner's horizon is broader and the areas of the state, the nation, and the world beyond are being explored. Thus such ideas as wants, consumption, production, and productive resources may become more abstract—not just the observations of children in their immediate environment but the wants of all people, the productive resources of the state, the nation, and other countries, in regional and international specialization rather than merely occupational.

In particular, the idea of a national economy can now be expanded. Students at this grade level should begin to learn the main characteristics of the American economic system and some of its institutions. They should learn about the role of money, about businesses and banks and unions, about competition, about the economic role of government, and about taxes. They should study the fundamentals of a market system, how consumers as individuals exercise choice and, in the aggregate, indicate to producers what is profitable to produce. To children of this age the parts of the circular flow idea—the total spending of consumers, the flow of goods and services from producers to consumers, the flow of productive resources to business firms, and the flow of income to households—can be explained. In short, in upper elementary grades students should acquire a knowledge of how the system of markets and prices, modified by government intervention, determines what, how, how much, and for whom goods and services are produced in the United States.

In the process of learning more about the central economic problem and about the characteristics of the American economy today, students will also have begun to acquire the "way of thinking" about human behavior referred to earlier—the perspective that is economics.

## Economics in Junior and Senior High

In junior and senior high school students study American history, civics, world geography, world cultures, world history, and the history of their home states. These courses provide almost limitless opportunities for the introduction of economic analysis. The task of the teacher is to identify the sections of the course that can be enriched in a meaningful manner by the introduction of economic themes. The task of both curriculum specialists and teachers is to plan the introduction of economic analysis into the six grades of junior and senior high in an organized way that will relate each grade's content to what went before, so that what is done in all grades will constitute a comprehensive plan.

When introducing economics into junior and senior high courses, there should be planned transfer of learning. Economic understanding means the development of a way of thinking about human behavior. What students need to learn, therefore, is how to use economic analysis in a variety of situations; for example, in the state of Washington growth since statehood is studied in the ninth grade. An analytical approach is used in which the ingredients of the growth process are identified, but the method of analysis, once developed, can just as easily be applied to another state, to the United States, or to a foreign country. Similarly, once the purpose of the market and the function of prices are understood, they can be used to interpret such economic issues as the stock market crash of 1929, the determination of foreign exchange rates, the regulation of public utilities, the monopoly problem, wage determination by unions and management, farm price supports, and the tight money crunch of 1969, for all of these economic issues are rooted in market situations.

Examples of appropriate introduction of economic analysis into junior and senior high school courses are: other economic systems into world history, international trade and the growth problems of underdeveloped countries into world geography, the economic role of government, including monetary and fiscal policy, into civics, and the principal characteristics and evaluation of the American economy into American history.

Often the same topic will receive different emphasis in different grade levels. For example, in eighth-grade American history, when economic growth is discussed in the context of our nation's development, the ingredients of growth, that is, the contributions to growth made by natural resources, immigrants, foreign capital, education, inventions, and the role of the government in encouraging agriculture, are emphasized. In eleventh-grade American history, however, the more complex problem of maintaining aggregate demand can be developed, for example, the role of money and banking and the effect of depressions on growth.

When students have completed the eleventh grade, they should have learned to use economic analysis in the areas identified earlier and in many of them more than once. More important, they should have developed the skills of using the tools of economic analysis in other problem-solving situations. The payoff will be a continued ability to approach complex economic problems in an analytical way long after they have left high school.

## Twelfth Grade Economics

In the twelfth grade students should receive their capstone experience in economics. In an increasing number of schools this is a separate course. In other schools it is a series of well-structured units in a problems of democracy or American problems course.

What is taught in the twelfth grade, and how it is taught, depends on what economics has been covered in earlier grades. In a school in which students have been exposed to economics in an organized way at every grade level since kindergarten, study in the twelfth grade can be relatively sophisticated. In schools in which this has not been done, or for those students who have acquired but few skills in economic analysis, the course is less sophisticated.

# 1

*Economic Concepts in the Primary
Grades K – Grade Three*

- **We All Have Wants for Goods and Services**
- **Everyone Is a Consumer**
- **People Are Producers**
- **Efficient Production Requires Specialization**
- **Resources Are Used in Production**

### Economic Concept I

*We All Have Wants for Goods and Services.*

1. Goods include clothes, toys, houses, food, furniture, automobiles, highways, and bridges.
2. Services include haircuts, laundry, concerts, television repairs, teaching, street cleaning, garbage collection, and police protection.
3. Choices among alternative goods and services must be made: a child with 25 cents cannot buy all the ice cream, balloons, and comic books he may want; most families cannot buy as much clothing, food, and furniture or have the quality of housing or cars as they might want, and even communities working together cannot provide all the education and other public services that people want.

In Minneapolis the first approach to understanding Economic Concept I begins in kindergarten. In later grades it is repeated with more complexity and with the discovery of more relationships to other aspects of the economy. See Example 1-1, p. 71.

First graders in the State of Washington study the conflict between never-ending wants and limited resources in much the same manner as those in Minneapolis. In this grade there is an understanding of opportunity cost, but no attempt is made to ask first graders to verbalize the idea. See Example 1-2, p. 72.

## Economic Concept II

*Everyone Is a Consumer*

We all use goods and services. Some consumption is individual—for example, wearing one's own clothes. Other consumption is collective —either private, as a family living in one house, watching TV, and using the family car, or public, as children in a classroom receiving a teacher's instruction.

First graders in Quincy, Massachusetts, learn the simple terminology that is basic to an understanding of Economic Concept II, as illustrated in Example 1-3, p. 73.

Kindergarten teachers in Des Moines, Iowa, use simple sketches to illustrate the idea of public consumption. See Example 1-4, p. 74.

## Economic Concept III

*People Are Producers*

Goods and services must be produced and many people—carpenters, farmers, automobile workers, roadbuilders, barbers, teachers, and policemen—are producers.

Production is organized in households in which members prepare food, manage money, make repairs, and take care of clothes.

Production is organized in businesses like grocery stores, dairy farms, newspaper stands, automobile manufacturers, lumber mills, and telephone companies.

Production is organized in government agencies like school districts, water-supply systems, sanitation departments, parks and recreation centers, public transportation authorities, and public construction programs.

Third graders in Oregon schools are assigned activities to extend the idea of organizing production to include the public sector. See Example 1-5, p. 75.

## Economic Concept IV

*Efficient Production Requires Specialization*

Production is more efficient when there is specialization—when there is a division of household chores among family members, commitment of a business to particular goods or services, and concentration of a government agency on special tasks.

Producers must make choices of products and services to be provided and the resources that will be used to supply them. A plot of land cannot serve both as a factory site and a playground.

First graders in Quincy, Massachusetts, are assigned activities to help them understand and apply Economic Concept IV. In the excerpt from the Quincy, Massachusetts, teacher's guide a beginning is made toward an understanding of optimizing in the use of resources. See Example 1-6, p. 76.

A more complicated study of specialization is shown in the excerpt from a third-grade unit in Richmond, Virginia. See Example 1-7, pp. 77–78.

## Economic Concept V

*Resources Are Used in Production*

Resources are people who help to make things or to provide services. Resources are things of nature—land, minerals, water, and air. Resources are also man-made means of production—airplanes, trucks, tools, school buildings, factories, and machinery.

Third graders in a history unit in Quincy, Massachusetts, study changing ways of utilizing land, labor, and capital. See Example 1-8, p. 79.

First graders in the State of Washington learn to recognize the production of goods in the home and to identify other workers who produce goods and services. The illustration from the Washington Teacher's Guide is taken from a second-grade unit. It is intended to extend student understanding to include organization of production. See Example 1-9, p. 80.

Second-grade students in the State of Washington use role playing as a culminating activity in comprehending the nature of resources. See Example 1-10, p. 81.

**Some TEACHING—LEARNING ACTIVITIES designed to develop the economic understandings within this unit—working and playing at school**

**Emphasis:** Conflict between never-ending wants and limited resources.

When the opportunities arise, children can be led to realize that each of us wants more than we can possibly have. We want more turns at the easel, more time for singing, more money to spend, and many things we never have at all. This is a problem because it takes workers, time, materials, and money to produce the things we want, and there are never enough of these resources. We must determine how to use our resources best to satisfy the most wants. This understanding can be illustrated and strengthened throughout the year.

**For example:** We want the janitor to heat the building, cut the grass (shovel the snow), raise the flag, empty the wastebasket, clean the bathrooms, and sweep the floors. He has a limited amount of time. So we choose to have the children in our school keep litter off the playground and pick up things on their classroom floors. We don't want to spend the janitor's time in this way.

**For example:** We have so many materials with which to work in kindergarten. We have paper, paint, toys, clocks, phonograph records, rhythm instruments, dollhouse, and books. The school spends a lot of money for these things, but it cannot have all the money it wants. If we want to add something new to our classrooms, we must use the things we now have carefully and make them last as long as we can.

**For example:** Sometimes we give up using something now so that we can have it for another purpose later. (This is the principle of saving.) When the occasion arises (whether it is paper, paint, or time), the teacher can help children to understand that we save now so that we can have more at a later time.

In one school, the children watched the glazier replace the many broken windows. They discussed his special skills and tools. They also talked about the expense and waste of energy and time necessitated by thoughtless treatment of property

---

Resources:
Book: *Two Is a Team*, Beim
Film: "Taking Care of Things"

---

Example 1-1 *Economic Education, A Supplement to the Social Studies Guide, Kindergarten, First Grade, Second Grade,* Minneapolis, Minn., Minneapolis Public Schools, 1967, p. 17.

| Children's Interpretation | Activities |
|---|---|
| The real cost of the thing we choose is the thing we must forego. | Have each child make a picture of a toy on a piece of 6"x6" tagboard. Display the pictures in a pocket card holder. |

Follow-up questions:

Which toy would you choose?
Why did you choose that toy?
What would your second choice be?
Which was easier to go without?

Stories:

Hunnicutt, C. W., and Grambs, J. D., *We Live With Others*.
"New Shoes," pp. 22-26
Galdone, P., *The Three Wishes*.

| | |
|---|---|
| Each person is free to decide which goods and services he will buy. | Provide a "Showing Day" for the children when they may bring toys and hobbies to school. As the children display their things, ask them to tell how and why they chose them. Would they choose their toys again or would they make another choice? |
| Every family must have a home, food, clothing, and must pay taxes. | Ask the children to name the goods a new baby in the family would need. Which items must the baby have? Draw out the general terms: food, clothing, home. |

Example 1-2 *Economic Education for Washington Schools, Kindergarten Through Grade Six*, Olympia, Wash., Department of Public Instruction, 1966, p. 3.

**Economic Concept:** Every family member is a consumer of goods and services but not every family member is a producer of goods and services.

| Economic Understandings | Teaching–Learning Activities | Materials |
|---|---|---|
| A producer is one who creates a good or performs a service. | Cut from magazine pictures of children illustrating work in the home. Have the children tell what is produced, who is producing it, whether it is a good or service. | Senesh, L. *Families at Work.* Chicago, Ill.: S.R.A., pp. 38–41. |
| Not all family members are producers. | Discuss: Do all members of your family produce goods or services? Who cannot produce? (baby, some other people depening on their age and/or health) | Provus, M. *How Families Live Together.* Chicago, Ill., Benefic Press, 1963. |
| A "consumer" is someone who uses goods and services. All family members are consumers of goods and services. | Review the meaning of "goods" and "services." Develop the meaning of the new word "consumer" (user). Help the children to see through discussion that they consume *services* as well as goods. Prepare the following seatwork paper for the children to illustrate: | |

I am a consumer. I consume goods and services. These are some of the goods and services I consume.

| Goods | Services |
|---|---|
| Drawing of food, clothing, toys, etc. | Drawing of mother sewing, mother cooking, father fixing bike |

| | |
|---|---|
| Goods consumed over a long period of time are called durable goods or "hard" goods. | Make a picture dictionary of goods that are consumed over a long period of time. Example: house, furniture |

Example 1-3 *It's Elementary—It's Economics,* Quincy, Mass., Quincy Public Schools, 1967, p. 11.

73

## Economic Dimensions

*Most people in a society believe that some of their needs and wants for goods and services can be best satisfied by having the government provide them. Taxes collected pay for these goods and services.*

**Suggested activity:** With the aid of a sketch similar to the one below, conduct a short discussion on the theme "what government provides us and where our taxes go."

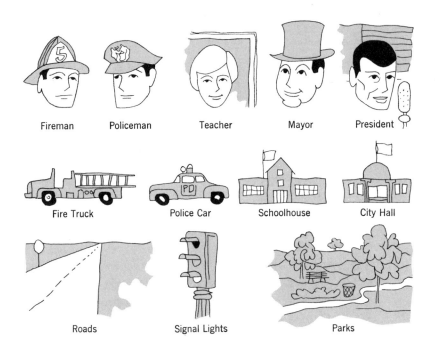

Fireman     Policeman     Teacher     Mayor     President

Fire Truck     Police Car     Schoolhouse     City Hall

Roads     Signal Lights     Parks

Example 1-4 *Goods, Services, and People, An Economic Sequence for the Primary Grades,* Des Moines, Iowa, Des Moines Public Schools, 1967, p. 9.

## There Are Government Agencies in Our Economic Area

**Supporting Concept**

Governmental agencies do not usually sell the goods and services they produce. They get the money that they need by collecting taxes from people and businesses. The people have to decide how high they want their taxes to be, what kind of taxes they want to pay, and which goods and services they want government agencies to provide.

**Vocabulary**

goods
services
local
county
state
property tax
income tax
sales tax

**Related Activities**

Play a game such as the following:
What if every family had to buy its own highway?
What if every family had to buy its own fire truck?
What if every family had to buy its own baseball field?

Have the children draw imaginative pictures about what would happen if government agencies charged for goods and services they now give away free. (What if the criminal had to pay the policemen? What if the pupils had to pay the teacher? What if people with fires had to pay the firemen?)

Have the children ask parents about the taxes they pay. List the taxes on the bulletin board.

Ask the principal to explain to the class where the school gets its money and what it is used for. Discuss whether the school could use more money. Do the taxpayers want to pay higher taxes so that the school can have more money?

Divide the class into federal, state, and local committees. Each committee reports on the taxes it receives and on the goods and services it produces. (Generally, property taxes go to local governments and schools; sales, income, and auto taxes to state governments; income and social security taxes to the federal government.)

Discuss why people pay taxes to hire people to tell them things such as—
"You cannot drive your car without a license!"
"You cannot build a house unless you get a building permit."
"You must send your child to school unless he is sick."
"You cannot have an unlicensed dog."
"You must obey the traffic light."

Example 1-5 *Teachers Guide to Economics in Grade 3*, Salem, Ore., State Department of Education, 1968, p. 30.

## The Home

**Economic Concept:** Division of labor usually results in greater *efficiency* and interdependence among people.

| Economic Understandings | Teaching–Learning Activities | Materials |
|---|---|---|
| A worker who does specialized work needs goods and services produced by other workers. | **Role Playing or Discussion:**<br>Child plays the role of mother. Mother goes to the sink to wash vegetables. She is getting dinner ready. There is no water! What will she do? She calls Father but he cannot fix it. What can he do now? Yes, he will have to call the plumber.<br>Story: Read the story about the plumber on pages 125 and 126 in *Science For Here and Now*. | Radlauer, R. *Fathers At Work*. Chicago, Ill.: Melmont, 1958.<br><br>Schneider, H. and N. *Science For Here and Now*. Boston: D. C. Heath, 1955. |
| Division of labor usually increases production. | Discuss: What would happen if all members of the family tried to do the same task at the same time?<br>Role Playing: Select four children to play the part of mother, father, brother, and sister.<br>Act I: All members are to do the same task at the same time:<br>    prepare breakfast    set table<br>        clear table    wash dishes<br>Act II: This time divide the labor:<br>    Mother prepares breakfast    Father sets table<br>    Brother clears table    Sister does dishes<br>Act III: Division of labor does not always result in increased production.<br>    Role playing: Setting table<br>    Three children selected to set table.<br>    First get spoons, second get knives, third get forks.<br>    Based on contrived materials.<br>    All utensils in one drawer. One child collects and distributes all eating utensils.<br>Discussion: Which is best? | Senesh, L. *Families At Work*. Chicago: S.R.A., pp. 42-47. |

76

Example 1-6 *It's Elementary—It's Economics*, Quincy, Mass., Quincy Public Schools, 1967, p. 17.

| Economic Understandings | Suggested Activities | Resources |
|---|---|---|
| **Human Resources** | | |
| 1. People are our most important resource. We must make full and efficient use of people in production. | a. Discuss the occupations of people in the community to point out the many different kinds of jobs that people have.<br>b. Have children choose jobs that reflect their interests and write short stories telling about them.<br>c. Discuss how skills and interests influence work done by members of the community. Draw pictures to illustrate people doing various jobs. | *Books:*<br>Puner, Helen. *Daddies and What They Do All Day*<br>Merriam, Eva. *Mommies at Work* |
| 2. People sell services and skills and receive income usually called wages and salaries. | a. Have children draw pictures and write stories about work they do in the community—running errands, selling papers, and raking leaves. | *Book:*<br>Beskow, Elsa. *Pelle's New Suit* |
| 3. Many different kinds of workers with specialized jobs are needed to provide a community with different services, food, and other products. | a. To emphasize the importance of specialization, the class might discuss how important to the community are such specialists as firemen, doctors, policemen, teachers, grocers, bakers, suit manufacturers, and drug manufacturers.<br>b. Discuss with children the importance of specialization in the community by using as examples the people who perform special jobs.<br>c. The children can ask their parents what they do at work and report to the class. Let them act out the jobs, if possible.<br>d. Members of the class can act out the activities of certain occupations while the rest of the class tries to guess what the occupations are.<br>e. List occupations in alphabetical order. A game can be played by the class using these occupations. | *Book:*<br>David, Eugene. *Television and How It Works* |

**Continued from previous page**

f. Invite a person whose work is concerned with manufacturing or food processing to tell the class about his work.

g. Discuss how the businessman, for example, grocery store manager, decides what products to place on his shelves.

4. Because work is divided, we must depend on other people to help satisfy many of our wants and needs.

a. Have children draw pictures showing all of the things that they would like to have. Let them write creative stories about their pictures. Then let them draw one picture of the thing they would choose if they had only one choice.

b. Read and discuss the poem, "The Balloon Man," by Dorothy Aldis. Point out choice and amount of money.

c. Have children make a class booklet using these title pages: "Things We Need," "Things We Would Like To Have," "Things We Could Do Without."

*Books:*
Kirn, Ann. *Two Pesos For Catalina*
"Three Wishes: A Swedish Tale," *Families at Work* (in our *Working World*), 72-73
Aldis, Dorothy: "The Balloon Man"

Example 1-7 *Economics Education, A Tentative Guide*, Richmond, Va., Richmond Public Schools, 1967, pp. 61-63.

## Foods—Then and Now

**Economic Concept:** Man has many more wants and needs than can be supplied by his available resources.

**Economic Understandings**

Methods of food production have changed since colonial days.

**Teaching–Learning Activities**

1. Show filmstrip: *Our Food and Clothing*. Only show the first part—food.
2. Discussion: Using corn as an example, compare the different ways of producing it, in early days and today.

| Steps | Early Days | Present Time |
|---|---|---|
| preparing land | hand plowing | machine plowing |
| planting | hand sowing of seed | machine sowing |
| fertilizing | fish | commercial fertilizer |
| harvesting | hand picked | combine |
| milling | hand grinding | machine grinding |
| by-products: | corn-on-the-cob | corn-on-the-cob |
| | ground corn meal | corn meal, corn bread |
| | or bread pudding | corn cereals, corn |
| products | or corn meal | chips, corn oil, margarine |

**Materials**

Bethers, Ray, *Perhaps I'll be A Farmer*. New York: Dutton, 1950.

Shannon, Terry. *About the Land, The Rain and Us*. Chicago: Melmont, 1963.

"Susannah Jane's Secret" *New Times and Places*. New York: Scott-Foresman, 1954.

"Judy's Chickens" "Maple Syrup Time" *More Times and Places*. New York: Scott-Foresman, 1955.

Example 1-8 *It's Elementary—It's Economics*, Quincy, Mass., Quincy Public Schools, 1967, p. 47.

79

## Private Enterprise

*Economic activity for the most part depends on private business firms.*

| Children's Interpretation | Activities |
|---|---|
| A business firm consists of men who make and sell goods to earn income. | List on cards in a pocket card holder as many different kinds of businesses of which the children can think. Suggest they look in magazines and papers, talk to parents, and observe businesses in the neighborhood for ideas. |
| A business firm may have many workers, a few workers, or just one worker. | Organize the name cards under these captions: A business with many workers. A business with a few workers. A business with one worker. |
| Some business firms produce goods or services to sell to other firms. | The businesses may also be classified under these captions: Businesses that produce goods for other firms (a machine plant, an airplane plant, a farmer who produces wool or grain, a cement, brick, or lumber factory). |
| Some business firms produce goods or services to sell directly to consumers. | Businesses that produce services for other firms (a trucking company, a railroad, the telephone company). Businesses that produce goods for consumers (food businesses, builders, factories). Businesses that produce services for consumers (stores, repair workers, transportation, professional services). |
| | Film: The City |

Example 1-9 *Economic Education for Washington Schools, Kindergarten Through Grade Six,* Olympia, Wash., Department of Public Instruction, 1966, p. 5.

## Production

*Business firms combine the productive resources of land or natural resources, labor, and capital goods to produce desired goods and services. In our system most business firms are privately owned.*

| Children's Interpretation | Activities |
|---|---|
| The business man needs a workplace for his business such as a store, factory, mill, or warehouse. He may pay rent to the owner or he may own his own workplace. | Discuss and list the different kinds of buildings used by businesses.

Explain that a businessman may buy a workplace or pay rent for the use of the land and buildings to the owner. Trucks and machines may also be rented. |
| Workers are needed to make the goods or perform the services. The businessman must pay wages to the workers. | List the goods and services a business needs:<br>A workplace.<br>Tools and materials.<br>Workers and a manager. |
| A manager may be needed to run the business.<br>He will be paid a salary. | Use role playing to develop a dramatization about starting a new business. Select one child as the businessman. Other children may be the landowner, workers, and producers of the tools and materials. |
| The businessman needs machines, tools, and materials to produce goods and services. | Have the "businessman" pretend to pay rent to the landowner, wages to the workers, and the cost of the tools and materials.

Note that a farmer is also a businessman who uses a workplace, tools, and workers

Classroom reference:<br>Senesh, L., *Our Working World:* Resource Unit<br>"What We Need to Go Into the Baking Business," pp. 146-150. |

Example 1-10 *Economic Education for Washington Schools, Kindergarten Through Grade Six,* Olympia, Wash., Department of Public Instruction, 1966 p. 7.

# 2

---

## *Economic Concepts in Upper Elementary Grades Four – Six*

- **Economic Systems in Other Nations**
- **Economics in State and Regional Studies**
- **Economics in American History**

In the upper elementary grades three areas of social studies are common to most school systems: Contemporary Societies of Other Nations, State and Regional Studies (history, geography, economics or special problems) and American Colonial History. In grades four through six it is becoming increasingly popular to extend economic perspectives, begun in the earlier grades, by analysis of the following:

- Economic Systems in Other Nations

- Economics in State and Regional Studies

- Economics in American History

### Economic Systems in Other Nations

The study of other nations in the Western Hemisphere is now common practice in upper elementary grades and a recent trend in this area is to question the following:

*Why Study a Particular Country or Countries?*

In looking for the answers schools have turned to the use of important major understandings from other disciplines to examine economic, political, or social patterns. Thus the newer practices seek answers to these and similar questions about the economic systems of other countries:

What are some contrasting resources (land, labor or capital) in selected countries?

How are these resources allocated?

How is production organized?

How are goods and services allocated to satisfy human wants?

In Minneapolis sixth-grade social studies have a unit on Latin America which includes a section that develops a theme in which the combination of people and physical resources in South America produces many ways of life. An illustration of the analysis pursued in this unit is given in Example 2-1, p. 85.

In Washington State sixth graders study other Western nations, and economic concepts are related to the economic growth and other problems of underdeveloped countries. The interpretation of these concepts is illustrated in Example 2-2, p. 86.

## Economics in State and Regional Studies

In most school systems in the upper elementary grades a major unit is devoted to state or regional studies. Washington State developed a unit for fourth graders, based on seven economic concepts, to enhance a Pacific Northwest study. Example 2-3 illustrates how this was accomplished (see p. 87).

Contra Costa County (California) schools developed a regional study for fourth graders. The type of inquiry illustrated in Example 2-4 is representative of the unit (see p. 88).

Minneapolis developed a fourth-grade regional unit that analyzes interrelationships of human resources, land, and capital, the dependency of one industry on another, and the effects of change on further change over a 50-year period. Example 2-5 typifies the continuing theme: parts of the system are inseparable from the total economy of the upper Midwest and the nation (see p. 89).

## Economics in History

In a beginning study of Virginia and the history of the United

States the Richmond public schools have built on the understandings of economics established in the primary grades and the new concepts then introduced. These units include resources (natural, human, and capital), operation of a free enterprise system, role of government in a market economy, role of agriculture in the economic growth of our country, money and its function, function of banks, and international trade. Placement is at Grade 5 and Example 2-6 is a portion of the first unit (see p. 90).

American history at the fifth grade in the Quincy, Massachusetts, public schools is reinforced in each unit by the development of explicit economic concepts:

| Unit | Economic Concept |
|------|------------------|
| Exploration and discovery | Scarcity is the relative lack of resources to satisfy all the wants of man. |
| Establishment of a nation | The economic policies of a government affect the economy of a society. |
| Civil War period | Trade between local and regional areas; more scarcity of resources in some areas than in others. |
| Westward expansion | The economic policies of a government affect the economy of a society. |
| Present-day government | The economic policies of a government affect the economy of a society. |

Example 2-7 is an excerpt from the first unit (see p. 91).

A social studies supplement prepared by the Dade County, Florida, public schools is unique and does not fit into any of the three categories illustrated. It was developed to serve all grades and the eight economic topics included are wants, choices, consumption, work, money, production, the market, and modifications of the market. Each topic is developed at six levels of sophistication. Instructions for using the document appear in Example 2-8 (see pp. 92–93).

## Economic Systems in Other Countries

Why do markets change from time to time?

1. New sources or increased supply
2. Cheaper or better substitutes
3. Newly developed materials (synthetic materials could decrease demand for Brazil's rubber)
4. Crop failure

Why would a one- or two-crop economy always be uncertain?
Why is trade important to a nation?
Which countries are buyers of Latin American products?
What products do the Latin American countries import?

> Resources: *Understanding Latin America*, pp. 294-295. Story of Chile and nitrate production.
> *Living as American Neighbors*, pp. 404-405. Story of rubber.
> *In Latin American Lands*, principal imports and exports given for each country. See Appendix in this volume for trade information.

Consider Latin American countries as markets for one another. Recall the characteristics of land that would explain their relationships. Recall that one reason population centers are adjacent to coast lines is the difficulty of developing transportation.

Contrast this lack of trade among Latin American countries with the interstate commerce of the United States; for example, fruit from the various states whose natural resources give them an advantage in these products.

What about automobiles in Michigan, paper, printing, and electronics in Minnesota, steel in Pittsburgh? How does specialization, or the development of a particular advantage in one product, help not one state but all states?

Example 2-1 *Economic Education, A Supplement to the Social Studies Guide, Fifth Grade, Sixth Grade*, Minneapolis, Minn., Minneapolis Public Schools, 1967, p. 117.

## Economic Systems in Other Countries

*Economically underdeveloped countries usually provide only a low standard of living for their people. The people of these countries want economic growth but are hindered by, among other things, their lack of labor skills and capital resources.*

| Students' Interpretation | Activities |
|---|---|
| A country in which most of the people have a low level of living is said to be underdeveloped. The country must grow economically if the people are to improve their standard of living. | Explain that the United States is called an economically developed country because it has a high average annual income per person compared with those of other countries. Countries in which the average income is so low that most of the people have a low level of living are often described as underdeveloped. |
| | Review the class's definition of a low level of living. Call their attention to descriptions in books or periodicals of actual living conditions of the poor people in underdeveloped countries. |
| | Have the class discuss ways they think the poor people of a country could be helped. Help them recognize that there are so many poor people in an underdeveloped country that gifts of money, food, or clothing from the rich will not help them achieve a better way of life. Their productivity must be increased. Their capital goods must be improved, their natural resources must be developed, and, most of all, the quality of their human resources must be raised. |
| In order for the people in the underdeveloped countries to have a higher standard of living, the workers must earn more income. To do so they must become more productive. The capital goods, such as machines, that are needed to increase their productivity must be paid for out of savings. Since most of the people are too poor to save, these countries find it difficult to grow economically. | Ask the students to pretend they are workers in the country they are studying. Have each one write a story about what he produces, how much he produces in a certain length of time, and how he spends the income he earns for his family. Have them also describe some capital goods that would help them to increase their productivity. What would they give up consuming in order to save enough income to buy the capital goods? Discuss the practicality of the different plans. |

Example 2-2 *Economic Education for Washington Schools, Kindergarten Through Grade Six,* Olympia, Wash., Department of Public Instruction, 1966, p. 7.

## Entrepreneur

*The production and marketing of most goods and services is organized and carried on by private firms.*

| Students' Interpretation | Activities |
|---|---|
| Most goods and services are produced by private firms. The members of a firm who make the decisions about how to conduct the business are called entrepreneurs. These decisions include when to establish a new business, what productive resources are needed, and when to put a new product on the market. | Explain the main functions of an entrepreneur in a discussion of the responsibilities of the head of a firm. Use a firm with which the students are familiar as an example. Stress these ideas: The entrepreneur decides what goods are to be produced and what productive resources are to be used. He decides what machines and production methods are most efficient. He expects the business to make a profit but he takes a risk that it may not. Discuss these and other local entrepreneurs who contributed to the growth of business in the Northwest: John Jacob Astor, Dexter Horton, Dr. Maynard, Thomas Mercer, Henry Yesler, Daniel Bagley and George Whitworth |
| Some businesses are small and owned and managed by one person. | Have the class use newspapers and advertisements to find examples of businesses that are owned and managed by one person. |

Example 2-3 *Economic Education for Washington Schools, Kindergarten Through Grade Six,* Olympia, Wash., Department of Public Instruction, 1967, p. 17.

**Content**

**Learning Experiences**

*Development*

If the class begins to complain that they cannot find much information on trade goods, ask the following *sequence* of questions:

Where did the missions get what they needed?

(mainly from mission production)

What did the missions do with what they produced?

(fed and clothed mission personnel)

Why did the missions not trade with the Indians who still lived in their own villages?

(little to trade, no advantage, and differences in cultural likes)

With the presidio soldiers?

(their supplies usually came from Mexico)

With the pueblo families?

(produced their own)

Why did the missions not specialize in cattle and send hides to Mexico?

(distance, Mexico had cattle, and the padres' purposes were not trade)

What is necessary for trading or selling goods?

(interest in making a profit, producing something someone needs, available markets, good transportation)

Read about the Spanish restriction on trade and the "moonlight markets" to avoid restrictions.

Suggested reference:

*California: A History,* pp. 138, 142-144
*California Yesterdays,* pp. 115, 123-127

**EARLY CALIFORNIA**

Example 2-4 *California Yesterday and Today,* Pleasant Hill, Calif., Contra Costa County Department of Education, 1966, p. 28.

**Main Idea:** Manufacturing and processing centers are located in relation to productive resources, markets, and transportation facilities.

1. Locate on the map the major businesses in our state:

| | | |
|---|---|---|
| Crystal sugar | 3M | IBM |
| United States Steel | Pillsbury | Northwest Airlines |
| Northwest Paper | Onan | Mayo Clinic |
| Hormel | Hamm's | University of Minnesota |
| Wilson | Brown-Bigelow | State capital |
| Honeywell | Green Giant | |

2. Let children explain why they are located as they are.
   Let them make hypotheses based on their understanding of the need each business has for land, labor, and capital (including raw materials).
   Help them to see the need for transportation facilities, market, water, and power supply.

3. Choose an industry that is located close to raw material (Northwest Paper) and one that is closer to market or labor supply and discuss why different advantages are more important to each.

4. Use story of the decline in flour milling in Minnesota to show how transportation affects the location of production.

5. A series of transparencies might be used to identify towns and cities of various sizes and the major reasons why each is important.
   The geographers characterize the present stage (1920 to the present) of city development as follows:
   - rural outmigration, growth of metropolitan areas
   - manufacture activities more important than primary processing activities
   - service sectors are of major importance
   - largest centers becoming increasingly important
   - large cities become markets for much of their own production
   - large cities are linked through air travel, freeways, and TV

Example 2-5 *Economic Education, A Supplement to the Social Studies Guide, Third Grade, Fourth Grade,* Minneapolis, Minn., Minneapolis Public Schools, 1967, p. 123.

**Economic Understandings**
**Human Resources**

**Suggested Activities**

1. Manpower is the most important resource. Human resources should be used efficiently.

a. Use current news to acquaint pupils with individuals who have made significant contributions to our economy's growth.

b. Invite selected persons to come in and talk about their work.

2. The quantity and quality of human resources are important.

a. Discuss and list qualities which increase the wise and efficient use of our labor resources. Example: good health, education, and knowledge.

3. Man applies ingenuity and knowledge to produce goods and services.

a. Encourage research by assigning oral reports on important persons and their contributions, such as Robert Fulton and his steamboat, the Wright brothers and the airplane, Henry Ford and his automobile, Alexander Graham Bell and the telephone, or Benjamin Franklin and the newspaper.

4. Division of labor and job specialization increase efficiency.

a. Set up an assembly line for the production of items, such as favors for Junior Red Cross. Show how individual efficiency is increased by each person doing a special job.

5. A large number of people in varying occupations work together to produce an article.

a. Read and discuss how fishing in New England involves the efforts of many people. View films on human resources:
*It Takes Everybody To Build This Land,* 20 minutes
*Story of Dr. Carver,* 10 minutes
*Meaning of Industrial Revolution,* 10 minutes
*Early Settlers in New England,* 10 minutes
*What Is A City?,* 11 minutes

Example 2-6 *Economics Education, A Tentative Guide,* Richmond, Va., Board of Education, 1966, pp. 120-121.

## Exploration and Discovery

**Economic Concept:** Scarcity is the relative lack of resources to satisfy all the wants of man.

| Economic Understandings | Teaching–Learning Activities | Materials |
| --- | --- | --- |
| Man develops ways of dealing with problems of scarcity through allocation of limited resources. | How did Columbus deal with the problem of limited resources (only three ships, insufficient crew, meager monetary supply, and poor equipment)? Elicit from class: higher wages paid to crew to solve one problem. Have one boy (Columbus) and girl (Queen Isabella) discuss reasons for using resources in particular way. Rest of class is court observing. | Recording: *Voyages of Columbus* "The Story of Columbus" *Living in the U.S.* New York: Macmillan, 1966, pp. 44-48. |
| Insufficient resources can lead to trade which may result in the interdependence of people, regions, and nations. | Role playing: arrange class in four groups representing areas of Europe, Asia, and Pacific Islands. Each group travels to a fair in caravans with their products to trade with men from another region.  Each group will offer for sale products and raw materials that the others lack. | Carls, Bacon & Sorenson, *In the U.S.* New York: Holt, Rinehart & Winston, 1966, pp. 421-426: 38-42. |
| Scarcity leads most men to desire, search for, and use substitutes for limited resources. | As a survey of the economic contributions of the early explorers make a chart of the English, Spanish, French, and Dutch explorers. List in the following columns:  1. What limited resources were they searching for? 2. What did they find? 3. Did they find a substitute for some resource in short supply? | Sanford, McCall & Cunningham. *You & the U.S.* Chicago: Benefic Press, 1965, pp. 46-55.  *Exploring in the New World.* "Finding a New World." Chicago: Follett, 1959, pp. 22-50. |

Example 2-7 *It's Elementary, It's Economics,* Quincy, Mass., Quincy Public Schools, 1967, p. 77.

91

This publication is designed as a teaching aid. It has been classroom tested and found to be effective in the teaching of elementary economics.

*Economics: A Social Studies Supplement* contains the following sections:

1. General introduction
2. Table of contents
3. Instructions
4. Overview of major concept (preceding each of the eight topics)
5. Overview of economic ideas (preceding each of the eight topics)
6. Teacher worksheets (in sections covering eight topics)
7. Bibliography (both general and by topics)

After reading these instructions teachers should be able to begin economics instructions immediately. Formal training in economics is desirable; however, by following this supplement, teachers will be able to provide interesting and meaningful learning experiences for students.

To become familiar with this supplement, it is suggested that each teacher read over the general introduction and the table of contents. This should be followed by a general scanning of the entire publication.

Actual teaching may begin by initiating the following:

1. Each major concept should be taught following with WANTS.
2. Turn to the appropriate level for your students. Levels run from one to six and are similar to grade levels. If a given level seems too difficult for your students, turn back to the previous level. If the material contained on the level selected seems too easy, move ahead to the next level.
3. When a given level is chosen for a topic, it usually helps to review the preceding level. This provides a background for the most sophisticated teaching activities contained in higher levels.
4. Each teacher worksheet contains four columns. The first is entitled Economic Idea and is simply a statement of the major point under consideration. The second column, Learning Objective, is a concise statement of what the student should be able to do after he has been involved in the Learning Experience, column three. The student's degree of success is ascertained by the assessment activity found in the fourth column entitled Assessment of Learning Outcomes. The teacher should read the column, Suggested Student Learning Experience, and have students follow instructions included in it. When students have completed their learning experience, they should be evaluated in order to determine whether the activity or learning experience has been successful in teaching the learning objective. In the event that the evaluation proves that students did not accomplish the learning objective, additional learning activities should be initiated.
5. When a teacher is in doubt about the level of capability or knowledge of his students, he may use the assessments set forth in the fourth column for pretesting. The results will provide information relative to the level of his students.
6. As students and teachers work

through the various objectives, it may be found that certain activities can be omitted or consolidated. If an economic idea has already been learned or if the teacher feels it is inappropriate. he should move on to more suitable activities.

Example 2-8 *Economics, A Social Studies Supplement,* Bulletin 9-H, Miami, Fla., Dade County Public Schools, 1968, p. III.

# 3

## Economic Concepts in Junior and Senior High School Social Studies

- **The Modified Market Economy of the United States**
- **Measuring the Performance of the Economy**
- **The Distribution of Income**
- **The United States and the World Economy**
- **Other Economic Systems**

The five major themes listed are developed in the junior and senior high schools. It should be noted that a major presupposition is made for all of the work at the junior and senior high school level: Students must be taught or retaught the basic economic concepts introduced in elementary classrooms. Even in a well-constructed developmental program it is necessary to review at various points such fundamental ideas as economic scarcity, opportunity cost, productive resources, and interdependence.

### The Modified Market Economy of the United States

In the American economy the basic economic decisions about what goods and services are to be produced and how they should be produced and shared are made by impersonal market forces, by those who have established positions of power in the market, and by the government. The basic understandings required are the role of markets and prices in economic decision making, private enterprise, the profit motive, and competition. Other understandings are the nature of the monopoly problem, the effect monopoly has on economic life, the policies followed in the United States with respect to the problem, and the economic role of government. Finally, it should be understood that one of the main features of our economic life is that our economy is constantly changing.

In the eighth-grade study of American history in the State of Washington schools all the above ideas and concepts are taught. Particular stress is placed on the changes in the economy that are continuously taking place, and which include the growing economic role of government, the growth of big business, the rise of organized labor, the industrialization and urbanization of the United States, and our country's involvement in the world economy. One section of the course is devoted to the way in which competition has changed in form over the years. Example 3-1 illustrates this section (see pp. 101–102).

In the ninth-grade social science course in the Pittsburgh public schools, the modification by government action of the market mechanism is taught under the title "Controlling a Market Economy." Important events in American history are used to illustrate that when goals other than profit must be achieved government action is usually necessary and this affects the market economy. The passage of the Pure Food and Drug Act, the Federal Reserve Act, and the Social Security Act, the clause in the Constitution which permits the Congress to collect taxes to provide for the common defense, and the establishment of the Tennessee Valley Authority are used as case studies. See Example 3-2, pp. 103–104, and Example 3-3, pp. 105–106.

In Granite School District (Utah) one unit in the twelfth-grade course, "United States Political and Economic Institutions," is called "The Role of Government in our Economy." The impact of government action on business, labor, and agriculture is examined, as are fiscal policy, natural resources policy, and policies toward international trade. The following section of this unit outlines a few of the conditions in the American economy that caused the government to establish a social security system.

1. The country was an agrarian society. People lived on self-sustaining farms, which one of the children inherited in return for providing for the parents in later years.

2. There was always some type of chore that even the most elderly could handle so that they always felt some usefulness and complete retirement was unnecessary.

3. Life expectancy was much shorter and the number of elderly was not significant.

Changes in living which have increased the need for a social security program include the following:

1. Life expectancy has increased (three times as many people over 65 today as in 1920).
2. Urban living has placed people in smaller living quarters where there is a substantial sacrifice in having your retired parents live with you.

In the twelfth-grade Course on "American Democracy" in the Pittsburgh public schools the functioning of the market mechanism is discussed, and a series of problems is presented to the student to help determine the "cost of allocating resources through consumer votes" (see Example 3-4, p. 107).

## Measuring the Performance of the Economy

How well an economy performs is partly determined by two criteria—growth and stability. Economic growth may mean that the total production of goods and services is increasing or that the total production per person is increasing. The first meaning is absolute and may be useful in any comparison of the industrial power of different nations. The second meaning relates to population growth and may be better for comparing efficiency and potential standards of living among nations.

Stability refers to keeping the economy on a steady course and avoiding inflation, deflation, and unemployment.

The performance of the United States economy is a major theme in eighth- and eleventh-grade American history courses in the Minneapolis schools. In the eighth grade *(U.S. Economic Growth to 1865)* the emphasis is mostly on the supply aspect of growth—capital formation, land expansion, and labor resources. Example 3-5 is an illustrative activity (see p. 108).

In the eleventh grade *(Economic Expansion in the United States Since 1865)* the Minneapolis guide develops the following topics:

The Record of Growth
Savings and Capital Formation
Specialization and Trade
Technological Change
Education: Backbone of Growth

Agricultural Productivity
Government Contributes to Growth

In each section the substantive issues are discussed in the context of American historical experience.

> The supply and demand sides of growth are developed in a ninth-grade supplement prepared by the Seattle public schools. History of the State of Washington makes up the social studies content area of this grade level, and the economics supplement enriches students' understanding of the historical development of the state. The resources of Washington in its early years, the changing resources, and the effect of new demands on growth are treated at a level easily comprehensible to ninth-grade students. Example 3-6 outlines some of the economic-growth problems faced by the people of that state as its economy continues to grow (see p. 109).

The Pittsburgh Public School System has published *Readings on the Great Depression.* The accompanying teacher's manual outlines the objectives of the following four lesson plans:

Recapturing the feelings and perceptions of the 1930's.

Understanding the ideological values of the times and the conflicts among them.

Knowing the relationships between the political and economic processes of decision making.

Analyzing the causes of economic instability and policies to cope with it.

Example 3-7 shows a lesson plan excerpted from the Pittsburgh material which deals with fiscal and monetary policy to combat economic instability (see pp. 110–111).

## The Distribution of Income

In a market economy people get paid according to the market value of the services they or their property render, modified by such things as minimum wage laws, social security taxes, and income taxes. Modifications by government have historically been introduced to benefit those who might suffer extreme disadvantage when their incomes are determined by the market—the very old, the very young, farmers, and minority groups.

> Attention is focused on the poor in the Pittsburgh student readings, *The Economics of Poverty.* Thirteen readings with photographs, car-

toons, and statistical data examine the characteristics of the poor, the war on poverty, and agencies charged with improving social and economic conditions: The Job Corps, Head Start, Vista, and others.

These readings are intended for ninth-grade students but they can be used at other grade levels. A special feature of the material is the parenthetical definition of difficult words and terms.

Reading 3, "The Distribution of Income," in Example 3-8, discusses the extremes in income among individuals; for example, Elizabeth Taylor is reported to have earned one million dollars for her acting in the film *Cleopatra;* many farm laborers earn little more than 1000 dollars a year (see p. 112).

Example 3-8 discusses the size distribution of income, that is, the percentage of families receiving various portions of the nation's income. Another important way of evaluating income distribution is by the portions that go to the factors of production:

How much in wages goes to labor;
How much in rents to landlords.
How much in profits to the owners of property.

This is called the functional distribution of income because it describes income by the function served by resources.

Functional distribution of income and its expenditures is one of the themes of Minneapolis' *Industrial Revolution for World History Teachers.* This guide also includes productivity and technological changes, savings, innovation, population, and the role of government. Although the purpose of the authors is "to help the student recognize the common requirements for economic growth and development," the excerpt in Example 3-9 illustrates the distribution of income and its effect on the composition of output (see pp. 113–114).

Changes in what consumers want to buy is a major explanation why some industries prosper and others decline, why some people's incomes rise and others fall. One of the most striking illustrations of this phenomenon is in American agriculture.

Agriculture is one of the areas included in Minneapolis' United States History supplement for eleventh-grade teachers, *Economic Expansion in the United States since 1865.* The text portrays graphically the increase in agricultural efficiency, the decline in farm population, and the relative decline in the proportion of consumer income devoted to spending on food. Example 3-10 presents a table and questions for students to show the relation of consumer spending to agriculture (see p. 115).

## The United States and the World Economy

The major ties connecting the American economy with economies of other nations are represented by the large volume of United States exports and imports.

The Downey, California, Unified School District has developed a series of capsule studies which contain major economic ideas, one of which is "International Trade—Why do Nations Trade?" This study places trade in the context of seventh-grade social studies. The activities listed in Example 3-11 stress the historical development of trade in the United States and also the advantages and disadvantages of international trade. *Minneapolis Trades with Japan,* a supplement to seventh-grade geography, divides its teacher's guide into the following sections: The Mechanics of International Trade, Basic Concepts to Build Upon, Development Problems of Eastern Hemisphere Countries, and The Economic Growth of Japan. Example 3-12 is a case study which shows the importance of Japanese-American trade, the industries involved, and how this trade benefits the economy of Minneapolis (see pp. 116 and 117–118).

## Other Economic Systems

Every country faces the central economic problem of how to use scarce resources to satisfy wants. Throughout history, in different ways, societies have approached the problems of what, how, how much, and for whom to produce. Contemporary societies also differ in the degree of reliance on the market mechanism in basic decision making and in the amount of planning. As more fully explained in Chapter 7 of Part One, most countries today are mixed economies in which some decisions are made in the market and others by central authority.

A study of an economic system in which the mix is heavily weighted toward government allocation of resources is included in a seventh-grade unit on the Soviet Union prepared by Seattle public schools. Example 3-13 illustrates how this is handled (see p. 119).

A more sophisticated treatment of comparative systems has been developed by the Pittsburgh public schools for a twelfth-grade unit in American democracy. Example 3-14 (pp. 120–121) is an excerpt from the teacher's manual which is keyed to student readings. The seven readings for this unit are
- A Command Economy: Planning
- Carrying Out the Plan
- Soviet Goals and Objectives

- Modifying a Command Economy
- Comparing Economic Systems: Statistical Data
- Comparing Economic Systems
    "Questions and Answers on Soviet Life"
    "How Russia Really Lives"
    "A Day in People's Court"
- Mixed and Changing Economies

An illustration of how an earlier economy operated in the Western Hemisphere places emphasis on the necessity for system. Example 3-15 is an excerpt from an eighth-grade unit on Colonial economy developed by the Atlanta and Fulton County, Georgia, schools (see p. 122).

## Economic Understandings

*Rise of Organized Labor*

In some labor markets, unions have organized the workers and bargain on their behalf with employers over wages and working conditions. In such cases, the agreements arrived at through collective bargaining are partially substituted for decisions made by the free market.

*General Consequences of Modifications*

Modification of the free-market mechanism has resulted in more "administered pricing" and monopoly problems as economic decisions are made by those with economic power; for example, government agencies, big business, and big unions.

*Changing Nature of Competition*

A decline in the traditional kind of competition was characterized by large numbers of sellers, freedom of entry into industry, identical product, and flexible prices.

There has been a rise in new kinds of competition:

Competition among substitutes

## Illustrations

Some reasons why labor has found it necessary to organize:

The need to equalize bargaining power with big business.

The Knights of Labor were organized in 1869, the A.F.L., in 1886, and the C.I.O. in 1938. The A.F.L. and the C.I.O. merged in 1955.

The desire for more industrial democracy by direct participation by the workers in decision making in their places of employment and in the economy as a whole. The labor movement helped bring about state child-labor laws, the establishment of the Department of Labor in 1913, and the Fair Labor Standards Act of 1938.

Examples of modification of the market system:

Farm price supports
Minimum wage law
Interstate Commerce Commission
Civil Aeronautics Board
Washington State Utilities and Transportation Commission
National Labor Relations Act (Wagner Act)
Sherman Antitrust Act

Consider the number of different kinds of every product that are available now in contrast to the limited choices of earlier times. Some industries, such as automobile, steel, or aircraft require such huge capital outlay that only a few sellers can enter the field.

Trains have been withdrawn from service as plane flights increase, nylon replaces silk, oleo can substitute for butter, color television is beginning to replace black and white, and aluminum is being used in products that were formerly made of steel.

| Economic Understandings | Illustrations |
|---|---|
| Competition for the consumer's "discretionary dollar" | Resort hotels and power tool manufacturers compete for the worker's "vacation dollars." |
| Competition within the firm | Buick and Oldsmobile compete even though they are part of General Motors. Colgate-Palmolive produces competing toothpastes and soaps. |
| Competition through innovation (non-price competition) | Automobile manufacturers install power steering, air conditioning, better radios, and power windows to appeal to buyers. Electric shaver manufacturers bring out cordless shavers. Supermarkets install bigger parking lots and provide carry-out service. |
| Competition through advertising | Companies compete by sponsoring television programs, creating catchy jingles to promote brand names, or using eye-catching packaging to get the buyers' attention. |

*Industrialization and Urbanization*

| | |
|---|---|
| The nation converted from a society of farmers and a rural population living in small towns and villages into one of industrial and commercial people living in large urban centers. | Some examples of the effects of industrialization are the following: Growth of manufacturing and trade in the Northeast between 1815 and 1860 Growth of cities during the nineteenth century Influx of migrant workers to industrial centers Invention of skyscrapers, street cars, freeways Movement of families to the suburbs Growth of megalopolis |

Example 3-1 *Economic Education for Washington Schools, Grades Seven, Eight, Nine,* Olympia, Wash., Department of Public Instruction, 1967, p. 12.

# Controlling a Market Economy
## Reading 23

In the American economy most economic decisions are made by the market. When the ice cream producer asks, "Shall I make more chocolate or strawberry, pistachio or butter pecan?" the market has an answer. When the plastics producer asks, "Shall I put my resources into hula hoops or plastic hose?" again the market answers. The supermarket manager asks, "Shall I stock butter or margarine, corn or peas, apples or pears?" The market answers, "Give the people what they are willing to pay for." As long as the goal is profit for some while making goods and services available to others the market comes up with answers that satisfy everybody.

The market fails to satisfy only when somebody decides that some goal is more important to him at the moment than profit for those who produce what people are willing to pay for. This does not mean that all market decisions are necessarily in conflict with goals such as social justice or economic stability. Neither does it mean that decisions that consider these goals are necessarily unprofitable. It merely means that the market has no mechanism for evaluating decisions in terms of goals other than profit. Some control over the market must be exercised by forces outside the market when market decisions appear to be ignoring important goals. Sometimes this control is exercised voluntarily; sometimes it is exercised by government.

Following are a number of events that occurred in America's past. For each event consider the following:

1. How would a decision dictated by the market differ from the decision described here? If the market decision had been acted on, what consequences might have been anticipated?
2. What goal was being protected by this decision?

A. In the early days of the twentieth century reformers were incensed by conditions under which meat was packed for distribution throughout the United States. Upton Sinclair wrote a best seller called *The Jungle* in which he described the unsanitary conditions found in meat-packing houses. The public was outraged. In 1906 Congress passed the Pure Food and Drug Bill. This bill laid down a number of conditions to which industries producing food and drugs had to conform.

B. Article I, Section 8 of the Constitution states: "The Congress shall have power to...collect taxes...to...provide for the common defense...of the United States...."

C. In 1907 a financial panic shook the American economy. At that time a great deal of financial power was concentrated in the hands of a few private bankers, but the government exercised little official control over their decisions. When Woodrow Wilson became president, he urged Congress to create a central banking system that would have the power to control banking activity. The Federal Reserve Bill, which created the Federal Reserve System, was passed in September 1913.

D. Following the Civil War forces combined to speed the growth of American industry. With industry, the American city grew and with the city, a class of people called the urban poor. When people who live in a city are poor they cannot grow enough food to keep themselves alive. They cannot even feed off berries from the forests. They must depend on someone else to give them food and shelter. Church groups frequently provided food and lodging for the urban poor. In 1889 Jane Addams, a well-bred young lady who had traveled extensively, became interested in their plight. She founded Hull House, a social settlement located in an old mansion on Chicago's west side. The west side had been an area in which grand homes had been built, but by 1889 it had become a slum. Hull House maintained playgrounds, club rooms, libraries, and kindergartens. It offered classes for adults, particularly immigrants, who as children had been unable to attend school.

E. For years people living in the valley of the Tennessee River experienced great poverty. Floods kept washing away the topsoil needed to grow food, and more than half the families in the area were on relief. Only two farms out of every hundred had access to electricity. Some felt that life in the valley would become reasonably comfortable if cheap electricity were available. Floods could be controlled, and industries other than farming could be developed. The investment needed to build a plant capable of providing this electricity was larger than private industries felt they could risk. The length of time it might take to realize a profit on this investment, if a profit were ever returned, was unknown. In 1933 Franklin Roosevelt called on Congress to create "a corporation clothed with the power of government but possessed of the flexibility and initiative of a private enterprise" to bring electric power to the Tennessee Valley.

F. The depression of the 1930's forced Americans to seek solutions to problems that had existed in less severe forms for many years. There had always been aged and unemployed with no means of support. In 1930 there were more. They were forced to go to private charities for food and shelter, but so many came that the charities themselves ran out of funds. Many were forced to the streets. Some begged. Some sold apples or pencils. Some stood in long lines for a bowl of soup, their only meal. In 1935 the Social Security Act, which established a plan for providing for the aged and the unemployed, was passed.

Example 3-2 *Economics Readings For Students of Ninth Grade Social Science,* Pittsburgh, Pa., Pittsburgh Public Schools, 1967, p. 77.

# LESSON PLAN: Reading 23
## Title: Controlling a Market Economy

*Subject Objective:* To indicate

1. that when goals other than profit need to be considered some outside control must be exerted on the market mechanism;
2. that in the American economy this control is frequently a function of government;
3. that when outside forces are used to control the market mechanism the economy is referred to as a modified market economy.

*Procedures:*

1. Have students analyze the goals protected by each decision reported in the events described in Reading 23. Encourage them to consider the alternatives available and the consequences that might be anticipated with each.

*Explanation of Purpose*

The alternatives here are to permit unsanitary conditions to exist in the food and drug industries and, on occasion, suffer the disease, illness, and death that might result or to ask those involved to eliminate the abuses voluntarily. The government's objective here is to protect the general welfare from the greed of a few individuals who might be tempted to put their profit above the risks to others.

Here the government is providing a necessary service that is unprofitable for private enterprise to provide. Defense is a service to the community that promises no profit. It might be pointed out that the government provides other such necessary but unprofitable services such as fire protection, police protection, and the operation of lighthouses.

Here the government's objective might be described as financial stability. Although a stable economy is profitable for most, a few can profit from instability or conditions that become a threat to stability. If these few have great power in the financial community, only the government has sufficient power to control them.

In 1899 social work would not have appeared profitable from the point of view of the market. Although in the long run improving the position of the poor creates a greater demand for goods and promises future profits, the market reacts only to the immediate profit picture. The goal of social justice moved Jane Addams to establish Hull House. Here individuals were voluntarily redistributing their resources and sharing them with the market's rejects. In this way they were restraining the free operation of the market mechanism.

Although certain economic activities may eventually become profitable, they require so great an initial investment that only the government can afford the risk. Yet the services may be essential for large segments of the population. The government has taken the responsibility of providing these services werever they have been judged necessary.

Here, also, the general public welfare is the issue. Again it could be argued that in the long run Social Security profits everybody, but once more it can be pointed out that the market reacts to the immediate, not the long-term, profit picture.

2. When all instances have been discussed, ask students if they can summarize the role played by the government in the American economy.

What you want here is a recognition of the subject objectives cited above. Introduce the term *modified* market economy and use this term in referring to the American economy whenever possible.

3. Have students suggest questions they might ask themselves to determine whether suggested government activities fall within the scope of the role projected for government in America's modified private-enterprise market economy.

Questions might include the following:

(a) Is the good or service essential?
(b) If it is essential, can it or will it be provided by the private sector of the economy (e.g., defense)?
(c) Is it essential for a larger sector of the economy than the market would provide for (e.g., education)?
(d) Can its use be limited to those who pay for it (e.g., air pollution)?
(e) If this good or service is provided by the private sector of the economy, will other objectives such as freedom, justice, economic stability, or economic growth be best served?

Encourage students to cite examples that show the relevance of the questions they suggest. Also have them apply the questions to their examples and give what they consider the answers to their questions. Then have them take the next step and state whether in their opinion their examples are a proper function of government in the United States. An example of such an analysis would be the following:

Student: "You should ask whether something is really needed. A fire department is an example of something that is needed. It might be run as a private business, but you can't take a chance on its not being there when you need it. Running a fire department is a proper function for government in a modified market economy."

Example 3-3 *Economics Readings for Students of Ninth Grade Social Studies, Teacher's Guide*, Pittsburgh, Pa., Pittsburgh Public Schools, 1967, pp. 75-76.

# LESSON PLAN: Reading 21
## Title: The Cost of Allocating Resources Through "Consumer Votes"

*Subject Objectives:* To know

1. that allocating resources through the market favors individual consumption items over the group consumption items;
2. that both methods of allocation have advantages and disadvantages;
3. that each instance has to be evaluated in terms of its own merits and the costs involved.

*Procedures:*

1. Discuss each of the following problems:

   (a) A device has been developed that helps to control air pollution. Do you think the decisions concerning the promotion of this device should be left to "consumer votes" or should its use be made compulsory by law?

   (b) The federal government's Office of Economic Opportunity has used some of its funds to educate consumers to alert them to the costs of certain business practices, such as buying on time. Do you consider this a reasonable expenditure of federal funds?

   (c) The number of cars that are sold determine the need for roads and parking garages. Meeting the need for adequate roads and parking has, in many cases, become the responsibility of local, state and federal governments. Is it reasonable to conclude that federal, state, and local governments should also have the authority to decide how many cars will be produced each year?

   (d) City parks and recreation areas are actually used by a very small percentage of the total population. In all fairness they should be built and supported by those who use them. Do you agree or disagree with this point of view?

*Explanation of Purpose*

Encourage each student to examine each situation in terms of the advantages of public control as well as its disadvantages. In each instance the student should be asked to decide which form of control he would favor, public or private?

---

Example 3-4 *Readings in Economics for Twelfth Grade Students of American Democracy, Teacher's Manual,* Pittsburgh, Pa., Pittsburgh Public Schools, 1968, p. 47.

Have students complete the following chart. They should place in the proper squares the number corresponding to the numbered possibilities below. If introducing a better machine improves the qualify of capital, then a 1 should be placed under capital, across from quality. The correct responses are indicated in parentheses.

Actions taken:
1. A better machine is introduced.
2. A worker uses more skill in operating a tool.
3. Two machines are added.
4. A drainage ditch is added to land.
5. More workers are added.
6. On-the-job training is given.

|  | Capital (1) | Labor (2)    (6) | Land (4) |
|---|---|---|---|
| Quality | | | |
| Quantity | (3) | (5) | ///// |

Quantity of land (natural resources) is fixed. Some land, like forests and fisheries, is restorable. Some, like mineral sources, when once used are gone forever.

This problem might be used as a little quiz to check understanding of the changes in the factors caused by technological changes.

Example 3-5 *United States Economic Growth to 1865, A Supplement for Eighth-Grade American History,* Minneapolis, Minn., Minneapolis Public Schools, 1967, p. 11–13.

## Problems of Economic Growth in Washington State

*Economic growth is a process that brings benefits to the people in the form of rising living standards, but it is also a process that creates problems. Most of them stem from the fact that growth means change and change imposes on people and on a society the necessity of making adjustments that are sometimes painful. What kinds of economic problems do the people of Washington have to face as the economy of the state grows? What kinds of decisions must they make as they seek to resolve these problems?*

| Economic Understandings | Illustrations |
|---|---|
| How many productive resources shall be allocated in the years ahead to the production of goods and services for private consumption, such as autos, television sets, clothes, and how many to goods and services for public consumption, such as schools, hospitals, and highways? This choice is important to citizens as it raises the question of how much will be taken from them in taxes and spent for them by federal, state, and local government. | Have the class discuss the need for new schools in the community as population grows, how much they cost, and what this means in terms of property taxes for local home owners. A discussion of the state's needs for highways, universities, and state parks and what they mean in terms of state taxes may be useful. |
| Growth is characterized (and in part made possible) by rapidly changing technology. Some skills and some business activities become obsolete; the demand for others expands. What happens to those people with skills we no longer need? How can businesses adjust to new types of production? How can we be sure that young people entering the labor force have the skills required to fit them into the new technology? To what extent can we rely on the market to make the necessary adjustments? To what extent must we "engineer" adjustments by means of government programs? | The supermarket replacing the corner grocery store; automatic machinery unloading coal cars in place of crews of workers. In attempting to answer some of the complex problems that have been posed, consider the following: Responsibility of individuals to seek education so that they can find a useful role in our economy. Support of training programs by *Private industry* and *unions*—Boeing, Lockheed. *Local government*—vocational education in high schools and community colleges. *State government*—state teachers' colleges. *Federal government*—Job Corps. |

Example 3-6 *Economic Education for Washington Schools, Grades Seven, Eight, Nine,* Olympia, Wash., State Department of Public Instruction, 1967, p. 13.

# LESSON PLAN
## The federal government copes with the problem of unemployment relief

*Subject Objectives:* To know

1. that there are two basic ways in which the federal government can affect the rate at which spending takes place: one is called monetary policy, the other, fiscal policy;
2. that monetary policy refers to the federal government's policy with respect to the supply of money created through bank credit;
3. that fiscal policy refers to the actions of the federal government with respect to spending, taxing, and managing the national debt.

*Skill Objectives:*

1. To develop some skill in using simple analytical tools of economics.
2. To practice their skill in identifying evidence that supports a generalization.

*Procedures:*

1. How can the federal government affect total spending?

Review the concepts outlined in the introduction to Section IV of the case study. In preparation for this lesson, you may want to expand your understanding of monetary and fiscal policy by referring to an introductory economics text.

2. It has been said that the major reason for the breakdown of state and local attempts to cope with the unemployment problem created by the depression of the 1930's was, in the case of local government, the dependence on property taxes and in the case of the state, constitutional barriers to the creation of tax devices capable of tapping sufficient resources to handle the problem. One could argue that even if these tax barriers had not existed, local and state governments would still have been unable to do the job because they have no real power over the banking and monetary system and without that power, economic stability cannot be maintained. Do you think this is so? Do you think taxes should have been raised in the 1930's?

Have students identify evidence that supports the generalization:

"Local attempts to cope with the unemployment problem were doomed to failure because of the city's dependence on property taxes."

Were there other reasons for Pittsburgh's failure to provide adequately for the unemployed? Should taxes have been raised? Now identify evidence that supports the generalization:

"The state's attempts to cope with the unemployment problem were thwarted by constitutional limitations to adequate taxing powers."

Can you suggest other reasons for the state's failure to handle the problem adequately? Should taxes have been raised? If taxes were not raised, how else might government spending have been financed?

110

3. Go through the decisions of the federal government listed in Section IV of the case study. Which of these actions would the state, even on a limited basis, be unable to take? To what extent do you think this would limit state effectiveness in dealing with the problem of maintaining economic stability?

Get students to identify which of the decisions involved monetary policy; which involved fiscal policy. Keep reviewing the anticipated effects of each policy, all else remaining constant, and the order of magnitude of the action compared with the order of magnitude of the problem.

Example 3-7 *The Economics of Poverty, Teacher's Manual,* Pittsburgh, Pa., Pittsburgh Public Schools, 1968, pp. 14, 15.

## The Distribution of Income

Although Elizabeth Taylor's income reflects the scarcity of "Elizabeth Taylors" relative to the demand for them, the size of her income also reflects the wealth of the economy. If the American economy produced only one million dollars worth of goods a year and paid only one million dollars for the resources needed to produce those goods, Elizabeth Taylor could not be paid a million dollars to make a single picture. Nobody would have the price of admission to see the picture. For Elizabeth Taylor to earn a million dollars for a single picture, the economy must produce considerably more than a million dollars worth of goods a year.

In 1965 the United States had a national income of 559 billion dollars. After Elizabeth Taylor was paid her million there was still 558,999,000,000 dollars left to divide among the rest of the population. This made it possible for many people to buy tickets to Elizabeth Taylor movies.

In 1965 there were 48 million families in the United States. If each had received an equal share of the United States' 559-billion-dollar national income that year, each family would have received more than 11,000 dollars. As you know, the income was not divided equally. The heads of most of those 48 million families went out on various markets and competed for their shares. Some got a big share and some found they had nothing to sell that anybody wanted to buy. Table II shows how income was distributed among the 48 million American families in 1965.

### TABLE II
### FAMILIES BY INCOME LEVELS IN 1965*

| Income Level | Number of Families (millions) | % of All Families This Number Represented |
|---|---|---|
| All Families | 48 | 100 |
| Under $3,000 | 8 | 17 |
| Between $3,000 and $5,000 | 8 | 16 |
| Between $5,000 and $7,000 | 9 | 19 |
| Between $7,000 and $10,000 | 12 | 24 |
| Between $10,000 and $15,000 | 8 | 17 |
| Between $15,000 and $25,000 | 3 | 6 |
| $25,000 and over | ¾ | 1½ |

*Source: U.S. Bureau of the Census, 1966.

1. How many families in the United States earned incomes of more than $25,000 in 1965? What percent of American families does this number represent?
2. How many Americans were living in poverty in 1965?

Example 3-8 *The Economics of Poverty*, Pittsburgh, Pa., Pittsburgh Public Schools, 1968, p. 13.

## Classroom Activities

To demonstrate the effect that consumer spending can have on the economy, reproduce a simplified input-output chart. Assume that the 60 percent which labor receives in each sector is equivalent to consumer spending. Assume further that of this consumer-labor income 60 percent goes for food, 20 percent for clothing, and 20 percent to hard goods. Draw in the basic divisions, but let the students complete the distribution that occurs as each sector receives payments. Each sector will pay out 60 percent in wages and salaries. That will be spent as mentioned above. The process goes on and on.

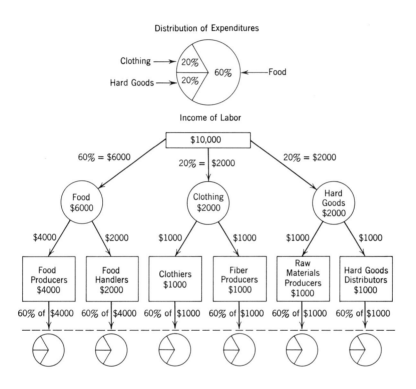

Distribution of Expenditures

1. Ask students to trace the 20 percent of consumer spending on the hard-goods industry to hard-goods employees' expenditures on clothing.
2. Ask students to draw in the expenditure that each industry makes to itself.
3. Ask students to draw in the next round of expenditures or possibly explain what they would be like, since each wave of spending gets more complicated.
4. Ask students to speculate on the composition of a similar 100-dollar expenditure by business and government. Hard goods probably would take more than 60 percent, and clothing and food the rest.

5. Ask students to make a similar breakdown of an expenditure by a factory for a new machine. How will the primary industry, mining, be affected? What effect will be felt by the transportation industry? How will the secondary industries, such as foundry, pattern makers, and designers, be affected? What will be the effect on the tertiary industry, manufacturing, on the distributors, and on the entrepreneurs all along the way? How will the expenditures of each of these recipients send the economy even further along?

6. For a description of the workings of this process in the American economy, refer to Clark C. Bloom's pamphlet, *How the American Economy Is Organized*. A Primer of Economics, Bureau of Business Administration, State University of Iowa, 1961.

Example 3-9 *The Industrial Revolution, A Supplement For Grade-10 World History*, Minneapolis, Minn., Minneapolis Public Schools, 1967, p. 18.

## PERSONAL CONSUMPTION EXPENDITURES

**Classroom Activities**

Examine the following statistics on personal consumption expenditures in billions of dollars (from the Annual Report of the Council of Economic Advisers, 1966, p. 219).

|      | Total Personal Consumption Expenditures | Automobiles | Food | Housing |
|------|------|------|------|------|
| 1929 | 77.2  | 3.2  | 19.5 | 11.5 |
| 1939 | 66.8  | 2.2  | 15.7 | 9.1  |
| 1949 | 176.8 | 9.9  | 44.8 | 19.3 |
| 1959 | 311.2 | 19.5 | 68.4 | 43.7 |
| 1965 | 428.5 | 29.9 | 84.9 | 64.7 |

1. Calculate what percentage of personal income was spent on food in each of the five years in the table.

$1929: \dfrac{19.5}{77.2} = \dfrac{x}{100} = 25.3\%$       $1959: \dfrac{68.4}{311.2} = \dfrac{x}{100} = 21.9\%$

$1939: \dfrac{15.7}{66.8} = \dfrac{x}{100} = 23.5\%$       $1965: \dfrac{84.9}{428.5} = \dfrac{x}{100} = 19.8\%$

$1949: \dfrac{44.8}{176.8} = \dfrac{x}{100} = 25.3\%$       (1949's increase over 1939 came because we were feeding wartorn Europe until its food production could be restored.)

2. What made possible these relatively reduced outlays for food? (Examination of the USDA chart *Per Capita Food Consumption and Disposable Income* will show that food prices have risen. However, the rise in food prices has been insignificant when compared with the rise in disposable personal income. Food expenditures have been kept low as a result of two things. First, with an already affluent society able to satisfy its food needs, little of additional disposable income is spent on food. Second, economies in food production have resulted from using more efficient inputs, as the USDA chart *Farm Inputs and Output Per Unit of Input* makes clear. Increased use of improved capital—machines, equipment, seeds, fertilizers, insecticides, and herbicides—and application of new techniques increased the output per unit of input. As output increased and as the effects of economies of large-scale production and new marketing techniques were felt, prices of foodstuffs were held to a minimum.)

Example 3-10 *Economic Expansion in the United States since 1865, A Supplement for Grade-11 United States History,* Minneapolis, Minn., Minneapolis Public Schools, 1967, p. 111-g.

# INTERNATIONAL TRADE—WHY DO NATIONS TRADE?

**Suggested Activities:**

1. Have students make export and import charts of the United States.
2. Compare exports and imports of the United States in 1850 with those of today. What changes have been made? Why?
3. Explore the possibility of what might happen to their fathers' jobs if exports and imports stopped.
4. Have students make a list of things that would be missing from classrooms if we stopped imports.
5. Make a list of the benefits individual nations gain through specialization.
6. List the pitfalls of overspecialization by nations or individuals.
7. Compare the standard of living and the amount of international trade of some of the nations they have studied in history during the year.
8. Investigate the role that trade played as a cause of the Revolutionary War.

Example 3-11 *Why Do Nations Trade, Teacher's Guide,* Downey, Calif., Downey Unified School District, 1967, p. 4.

Foreign trade has always been an important factor in the economic development of Japan.

Japan's earliest exports consisted of tea, fish products, and silk. Cotton textiles assumed importance around 1890.

Trinkets, toys, souvenirs, and an endless list of "Made in Japan" articles have become almost as familiar to the American housewife as those "Made in U.S.A." Many Japanese products are inexpensive novelty items. However, this is not true of other manufactured goods like sewing machines, cameras, transistor radios, grand pianos, and ships. Japan now produces heavy goods and fine instruments.

During the 1960's Japanese exports of chemicals and machinery have become relatively more important. Stainless-steel products are a good example of the goods coming into the United States.

## Summary

The change in the type of goods the Japanese manufactured for export is partly explained by the relatively high education of their labor force. This enables the Japanese to make the best use of technological improvements. Having the highest capital formation rate in the world is a second positive factor. On the other hand, how do we explain the decline in importance of the silk industry? This decline is due to the development of synthetic fabrics, coupled with the desire of underdeveloped nations to produce their own textiles. Japan was forced to turn to other products. Europe increased Japan's difficulties by refusing to take Japanese textiles in large amounts. It is therefore a combination of internal and external factors that determine the composition of Japan's exports.

## Classroom Activities

1. A large map of the United States and a large map of Japan might be mounted on the blackboard. Identify eight or ten industrial cities in the United States known for a specific product (e.g., Detroit cars, Pittsburgh steel). The students might be asked how people in Detroit made a living. Someone will surely mention cars and this can be identified as a principal way people in Detroit make a living. This discussion can proceed to industries and services that have grown up to supply the automobile industry (tool and die plants, paint, glass, plastics, transportation, and financing). A review of the factors necessary for production of goods and services is logical. Was our supply of these factors always the same?

   The teacher could move to the map of Japan. The children might be asked how they think the people of Japan make a living. After the students have given a number of opinions, the teacher might ask the students to check these guesses with the information in their geography books and encyclopedias. They can then make a picture map to show the important ways of making a living in Japan.

2. Using the information on the maps as a basis for discussion, the teacher might ask the children why they think the Japanese make their living as they do. Discuss the supply of land and natural resources—small; the supply of labor—large; the quantity of capital goods—small, but growing; and

business leadership—quasi-monopoly. Which factor is in largest supply? Which factor is in smallest supply? Does the fact that Japan has lots of people influence her methods of production? (many workers per machine.) How did she increase production? (By giving her people better tools and factories—capital goods.)

3. An excellent movie is available from the Visual-Aid Department of the Minneapolis Public Schools.

*Japan—Miracle in Asia* (EBF, color, 30 minutes, 1964-1965) gives an exceptionally fine picture of the industrialization of Japan. Here are some ideas to emphasize:

- All industrial centers are near the sea because Japan is a trading nation.
- Japan has to import most of her raw materials.
- Japan exports many of her products.
- Hydroelectric power is a highly developed and cheap source of power in Japan.
- Japan is a literate nation. Her labor force is able to use complicated machines and processes.
- The underdeveloped nations now produce toys, footwear, and textiles, the prewar products of Japan.
- Japan specializes in producing steel, ships, electronic equipment, motorbikes, cars, generators, and turbines.
- Japan spends little on defense.
- More than one-quarter of Japan's GNP is invested. This makes further growth possible.
- Japan is the first mass-consumer market outside the Western world.

Example 3-12 *Minneapolis Trades with Japan, A Supplement to Grade-Seven Geography*, Minneapolis, Minn., Minneapolis Public Schools, 1967, p. 26.

## Economic Understandings

In many ways the Soviet Union has applied communist ideology to its economic system.

The state (nation) owns all natural resources, all heavy industry and power plants, all railroads, ships, and airlines, all banks, all communications networks, the wholesale distribution agencies in the cities, and the great majority of retail stores. The government operates state farms and controls other farms which are technically cooperatives (collective farms).

No one is permitted to buy goods to sell at a profit or to employ labor for profit making.

Communist ideology applied to an economic system leads to a basically command system. Centralized decision making is the method used to determine what goods and services shall be produced, how much of each shall be produced, how they shall be produced, and who will get what is produced.

## Illustrations

What kinds of property are left for individuals to own?

Would this system of property ownership have any effect on how basic decisions regarding economic policy are made?

What differences would it make whether or not the people could express choices by voting?

Under such a theory would one-man shops, partnerships, or cooperatives be allowed? Why? Could large private businesses develop? Why or why not?

In the Soviet Union the amount of consumer goods such as clothes, furniture, appliances, and other household goods has been limited so that more heavy machinery, industrial equipment, and military goods can be produced.

Example 3-13 *Economic Education for Washington Schools, Grades Seven, Eight, and Nine,* Olympia, Wash., State Dept. of Public Instruction, 1967, p. 10.

## LESSON PLAN: Reading 36
## Title: Carrying Out the Plan

*Subject Objectives:* To know

(1) that planners must rely on others to carry out their plans;

(2) that those called upon to carry out the plans must be motivated;

(3) that all societies must motivate their people, either by coercion or persuasion, to carry out their goals.

*Procedures:*

*Explanation of Purpose*

1. Once a "plan" has been adopted by Soviet planners, what happens to it?

Encourage students to describe the process they envision: Gosplan prints copies of the final plan and distributes them to regional councils. Regional councils give detailed plans to each factory. Factory managers make arrangements to get the raw materials and labor they need to produce the quotas assigned them.

2. How are people encouraged to do what the plan asks of them?

Managers are given rewards such as better housing, a car, and paid vacations. Workers are frequently paid on a piece-rate basis. They are paid in terms of how much they produce rather than how long they work. Workers are also paid bonuses for extra production. In addition to positive incentives, negative incentives such as coercion have been used. Evidence seems to indicate, however, that in recent years the Soviet Union has found positive incentives more productive than negative incentives and is now relying much more on inducing its workers than on coercing them.

3. The piece-rate system of wages has been discouraged in the United States by labor unions who argue that piece-rates are used to exploit workers and keep their wages low. It was the contention of unions that as workers became more skilled and produced faster, rates per piece were lowered to keep wages from rising too fast. Do you think piece-rates are used in the Soviet Union to exploit Soviet workers?

Students should be encouraged to look at the decisions of others in terms of the goals of others. The fact that American labor unions accused American industrialists of using piece-rates to exploit American workers is no reason to assume that Soviet workers are being exploited by the system. The fact that piece-rates were adopted to motivate workers and increase total production would imply the opposite but it depends on whether the "rates" are changed and how these changes are made.

4. Your current "job" is going to school. One goal of the American society is for each student to do his "school work" and to graduate from school better prepared to do some job needed by the economy. How are you "motivated" to do the job asked of you by society? Is society's way of motivating you working? What types of motivation work for you? What types fail?

Students should recognize that all societies motivate the individuals within that society, more or less successfully, to carry out the goals of the society. Some societies motivate by persuasion, some by coercion, but most by a combination of the two.

---

Example 3-14 *Readings in Economics for 12th Grade Students of American Democracy, Teacher's Manual,* Pittsburgh, Pa., Pittsburgh Public Schools, 1968, p. 74.

# COLONIAL ECONOMIC SOCIETY

Let us take a look at American economic society in 1770. Our forefathers were preparing to rebel against a political policy of the British government—that of making economic decisions for the colonists without letting them be represented in Parliament. We shall create an economic model for looking at this Colonial society.

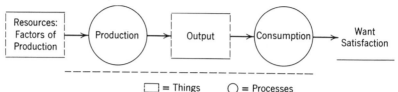

☐ = Things     ○ = Processes

General idea: all societies face problems of using resources (which are limited) to satisfy wants (which always seem to exceed the capacity to satisfy). In this model, imagine that our product is ice cream.

1. The resources consist of the ingredients needed to make ice cream and the labor, and capital (tools and equipment needed).
2. Production is the process of combining the resources to get our finished product—each society has ways of producing.
3. Output consists of all goods and services turned out by the production process. This means both physical goods such as hammers, TV sets, yard goods, and services such as an hour of teaching, a sermon, or a TV repair. In our example the output (or product) is ice cream.
4. Consumption is the process by which final output is transformed into want satisfaction—eating the ice cream, for example.

   It should be noted that some output would not move directly to consumption process but would be retained by the *producers* in the form of capital goods or semifinished products to be used in the process of producing still other outputs—for example, steel girders, bricks, glass used in autos, or a stove in a restaurant.
5. Wants Satisfaction consists of the feeling a person has when that particular want is satisfied—the pleasant feeling one has when he has finished eating the ice cream he had wanted.

Questions relating to the economic model as applied to Colonial economy:
1. What were some of the things early Georgians wanted?
2. Why did they not have all the things they wanted?
3. What did they have to do to secure the things they needed?
4. Do most people face the same problem of choosing?
5. What did they need in order to make what they wanted?
6. Can you think of any goods or services whose production does not require labor and capital and raw materials?
7. Could the colonial people have varied the amounts and quality of the natural resources needed to produce what they desired?
8. What would they have had to consider in making such a decision or decisions?
9. Why might one community decide to use their natural resources one way while another community makes a different decision?

Example 3-15 *Changing Culture, Social, Economic, Political,* Atlanta, Ga., Atlanta and Fulton County School System, 1966, p. 10.

# 4

# *Economic Concepts in the*
# *Twelfth Grade*

Most school systems offer either a required or an elective course in basic principles of economics at the twelfth grade or a unit of economics as part of a problems of democracy course.

In school systems in which the social studies from grades one through eleven have been enriched with economic understandings the twelfth-grade semester course in economics or the unit as part of another course may be designed as a culminating experience and economic understanding may be carried to considerable depth. On the other hand, in school systems that have not enriched the social studies with economic analysis at lower grades the twelfth-grade course is often an introduction to the subject.

Because of this distinction between economics as capstone culmination and as first experience, the course content outlined in the following pages is categorized under these two headings. It must be emphasized, however, that several of the illustrations for one kind of course are appropriate to the other; it is essential only that they be tailored to the needs of the students and the teacher's experience.

A few general remarks apply to twelfth-grade economics, whether it is capstone or introductory, about trends developing in the creation of economics courses at the senior high school level.

Courses and units in twelfth grade economics are becoming more *economical.* Instead of attempting the encyclopedic coverage that often typified these offerings, content and instruction are becoming more selective. Less emphasis is placed on the discipline's numerous applications in such problems as international trade, poverty, unemployment, and other areas often listed in the table of contents of a college or high school textbook. Greater emphasis is now being placed on the students' mastery of the key concepts of economic analysis and their application to fewer problems in greater depth.

Courses and units are becoming more *systematic* and what is taught is being more systematically related to the central ideas of economic analysis. The interrelationships among the principles of economics is emphasized and economics is being viewed as a single integrated body of knowledge with all its parts interdependent. This presentation of the discipline stresses the idea that the economic systems of the family, business, and nation are real-world counterparts of an intellectual system that is a single body of thought. This emphasis on the interdependence of systems is concomitant with the emphasis now being placed on the transferability of knowledge from one situation to another. Bruner* expresses this in the phrase *structure of a discipline* in which commonalities are stressed among diverse situations. This perspective avoids limiting economics only to its applications to particular problems.

Economics teaching uses *analogies*. Both the natural and the social sciences are composed of disciplines that are more or less single, unified systems of thought. Biology, for example, when viewed as a single perspective on the kingdoms of plants and animals offers a better appreciation for the other systems or perspectives like economics. Even though the forms of behavior are changed, biology exhibits almost all of the major ideas common to economic analysis. To illustrate: there is competition among species for the scarce space in which to live and for the scarce nourishment provided by the environment; division and specialization of function is no less common in biology than in economics; analysis of systems in equilibrium is common to both. By developing a few salient points from another discipline, whether it be biology, physics, or political science, the student can be helped to advance both his understanding of economics and other subject areas.

The teaching of economics is searching for what is most *relevant* to the social realities of the learner. Most striking in this connection is the attempt to close the gap between the image of the economy seen by the child in the ghetto and the image of affluence too often projected through instruction. The teacher and text may praise the market system's beneficence while the child's father cannot find a job; they may speak of the economy's ability to satisfy "unlimited wants" while the student hungers for a good meal, a pair of shoes, or a sense of identity.

*Jerome L. Bruner, *The Process of Education*. New York: Alfred A. Knopf, and Random House, 1960.

Instruction is now attempting to express a greater *awareness of values*. The myth that any natural or social science is free of values and must avoid moral judgments is gradually giving way to an explicit recognition of the need for value relationships. This has been frequently summed up in the idea that an economy produces both goods (toys and houses) and "bads" (air pollution, highway deaths and urban squalor). Only the value of the goods is presently added into gross national product. Admitting the "bads" does not mean a sacrifice of the goal of objectivity nor a confusion of ethics with economics. It does mean acknowledging the limits to economic analysis.

The material in the following pages is divided into two sections:

1. Illustrations of course content not dependent on a student's having studied economic analysis in the lower grades.
2. Illustrations of course or unit content built on some previous study of the subject.

There is great overlapping between these two sections and some of the illustrations for courses not defined as capstone or culminating may nonetheless be adapted to this purpose. The suggestions contained in the first section are not to be considered inferior or in any way deficient just because they are classified here as courses or units lacking capstone variety.

## Courses and Units Independent of a K-11 Sequence

Working with an advisory panel and with special consultants, Professor Norman Townshend-Zellner, assisted by Professor Sylvia Lane, prepared for the California State Department of Education a resource document setting forth a proposal for the teaching of economics at the senior high school level.* This document exhibits the current trends of the economy, systemic inquiry, and the analogical reasoning previously emphasized.

Townshend-Zellner and his colleagues John Lafky and Sylvia Lane had consulted extensively in the Developmental Economic Education Program (DEEP), especially with the Downey, California, schools.

---

*A Resource Document for a High School Course in the United States Economy, Sacramento, Calif., California Department of Public Instruction, 1967. Available from the Joint Council on Economic Education, 1212 Avenue of Americas, New York, New York 10036.

His direct experience with classroom problems is reflected in this resource document.

The following excerpt shows the intention of the author in developing this instructional guide:

School districts, curriculum specialists, and teachers can use this resource document to develop their own course outlines, instructional guides, teaching units on various aspects of economics, and instructional aids and materials. Specifically, this resource document should be of great value to all who have responsibility for the provision of instruction in economics for high school students since it will aid them as follows:

- To recognize and understand over 15 fundamental issues that must be handled and resolved in developing a course in economics for high school students. All too often, these issues are either ignored or simply treated implicitly. Yet they are the basic building blocks for an economics course and must be given full consideration in developing an instructional guide for such a course.
- To develop an approach to economics that is comprehensive and integrated, and, in addition, is organized specifically to highlight the major operations and problems of the United States economy.
- To use throughout the successive units a series of novel, simple diagrammatic models to integrate continuously the complex material of economics at all stages. Such simple, intuitive models are developed specifically in this resource document to provide the teacher, and in turn the student, with the simplest, least technical, yet most comprehensive tools of economic analysis.
- To develop simple verbal explanations and analyses, at the intuitive level, of information and ideas often presented in textbooks in the form of technical graphic analyses. The use of these by teachers to provide instruction will enable students who cannot profit from study of technical analysis to grasp the essential idea of how the United States economy operates.
- To develop "options in depth" that teachers can use with students who are qualified and sufficiently motivated to plunge increasingly deeper into technical analysis. However, the integrity and continuity of the material presented in this resource document is maintained if all "options in depth" are omitted.
- To develop intensive and novel uses of the comparative method in teaching "economics."

The author makes no attempt in this document to spell out learning experiences in detail or to present detailed outlines of all topics.

The subsection headings of Part Two of the California Guide, *Issues and Problems that Must be Resolved in Developing a High School*

*Economics Course,* indicate how comprehensive the authors have been in defining important curriculum issues.

- Use of a Content-Criterion
- Flexibility
- Student-Centering
- Integration-Unification
- Pruning and Cutting
- Functional-Discipline Orientation versus Problem Orientation
- Information and Description versus Analysis
- Sequence of Organization
- History of Economics and Economic Thought
- Myth-Breaking
- Methodology and Scope of Economics
- Relationship of Economics to Other Social Sciences and Philosophy
- Use of Programmed Learning Techniques
- Controversial Issues
- Role of Government
- Comparative Study of Economic Systems
- Graphs, Tables, Charts, and Diagrams
- Sources and Bibliography

Section 1 of Part IV of the California Guide, *Overview of Economics and Economic Systems; Synthesis of Model 1,* illustrates how the economic system may be considered an abstraction from the real world and why it is merely one subsystem among the many that make up our intellectual conception of social organization.

### THE ECONOMIC SYSTEM

What is referred to as "the economy" is simply the complete economic system, abstracted from the entire social system in which people live. This economic system is the abstracted "world of economics."

1. People actually live in an entire, unabstracted social system that comprises people together with all their activities, institutions, organizations, and environment (see the left-hand portion of Example 4-1, p. 128).
2. For study and understanding, however, almost without conscious planning, people tend to use the systems approach—to think about the entire social system in terms of basic subsystems, each founded on similar types of activities and decisions, and to carve it up along

127

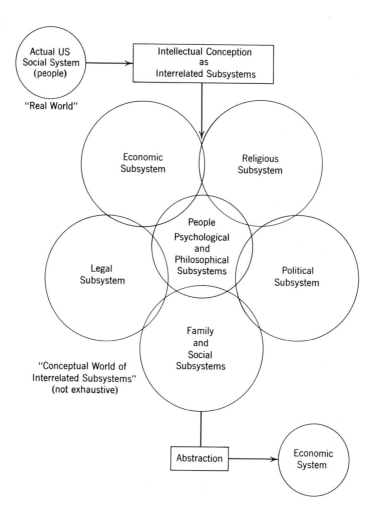

such lines for study. Each subsystem of the social system, when considered separately, may be called a system. The social system, then, is thought about in terms of such systems as the following:

a. Religious system—the realm of religion, religious activities, and religious decisions.
b. Government or political system—the realm of governments, governmental decisions and activities.
c. Legal system—the world of law, legal activity, and legal decisions
d. Social group system—the world of basic social groups, e.g., family activities and decisions.
f. Philosophical and psychological system—the world of people's values, ways of thinking, beliefs, attitudes; and so on

3. Each of these systems may be abstracted from the total system for study and understanding. For example:

   a. Political scientists study the political system.
   b. Economists study the economic system, its activities and decisions.

4. Thus, the economic system is nothing more than the result of an intellectual carving out of a particular kind of subsystem (consisting of economic decisions and activities) from the entire social system. The economy, as abstracted from the whole system, can then be studied as an entity (see right-hand part of Example 4-1, p. 128).

5. During study of the economic system, certain allowances must be made for the following facts:

   a. The economic system does not really exist by itself; an intellectual operation has created the idea of a distinct economic system.
   b. The economic system is affected by, and involved in, all the other kinds of activities and decisions of people—political, religious, social, legal, and psychological. These, in turn, are affected by and involved in the economic system.

STUDYING THE ECONOMIC SYSTEM—A FIRST MODEL

A model is an apparatus that explains and helps people (e.g., students, engineers, scientists) to understand the working of a system and that enables them to make the predictions about, or to control, the system.

1. Models are frequently used as aids to the study of automobile engines, traffic flow systems, or hydrogen atoms, for example.

2. Models are usually much simpler than the system they explain. For easier understanding, control, and prediction, models may omit the less important complexities of the system they represent.

3. Models need not be exact replicas of the system. Their main function is to contribute to understanding.

4. Models do not have to be physical in form. They can also be intellectual inventions, expressed in words, diagrams, or mathematics.

5. Essentially a model depicts the system's parts and their relationships. The model, as it were, tells the story of the system in a way that helps in the understanding of what otherwise might seem an enormously complex system. Economic models help one understand the economic system or the particular economic subsystems, that have been defined for purposes of understanding or of problem solving.

6. The United States economic system is so complicated that a large number of models are needed to provide means of understanding it.

   a. Simplified models of the overall system are needed.
   b. More detailed models of the various subsystems are needed.

c. Finally, an understanding of how all the different models fit together must be achieved.

d. A similar process is followed in areas other than economics. To understand the automobile, one may start with an overall model, including chassis, engine, body, and appurtenances; and then continue with detail models of an engine, a transmission, or other subsystem. To understand the human body, study can start on an overall model and continue with detailed models of the skeletal system, the circulatory system, and so forth. Further abstractions of subsystems may be used for more detailed study.

7. Since there are an infinite number of systems, there can be an infinite number of models. Models can be good or poor, depending on the skill of the maker. A model is poor when it does not help to explain how a system works or help to predict or control the system.

8. Models reflect the thinking, purposes, and system definition of the maker. Models are made by people; they are extensions of the thinking of specific people.

a. For example, a model showing the functions of an automobile made by an engineer would be much different from a model showing the styling made by an auto designer.

b. When models are used, care must be taken to detect any signs of ignorance or emotional responses that are built into the model. Through ignorance people may leave an important part out of an economic model; or through pure emotional reaction they may include a part that has no business being there. Models that reflect ignorance or emotional reaction are not useful tools of understanding, prediction and control—at least they are not as useful as they might be.

## ECON 12*

A special effort to develop a twelfth-grade semester course in economics in Contra Costa County, California, was conducted by Suzanne Wiggins and John Sperling from 1964 through 1968 as part of the DEEP program. The following quotations from Dr. Wiggins' 1968 report, addressed to teachers and other educators, gives the main characteristics of ECON 12. The author's emphasis on the course as a teaching system is worth noting.

ECON 12, designed for high school seniors, is an introduction to economic science and philosophy. It is written for the average

* Suzanne E. Wiggins, *A Report on the Use of ECON 12 in the Introductory Principles of Economics Courses at San Jose State College,* San Jose, Calif.: San Jose State College Economics Education Center, Dec. 1968.

American who has survived eleven years of public school education, to help him understand the economic dimension of his personal life and of his society, to help him learn to use this understanding to analyze contemporary private and public economic policy issues.

To build a good high school or college introduction to economics we think it is essential to overcome these two obstacles: (1) students lack of experience and disinterest in deductive model building; (2) the credibility gap between economic theory and its usefulness in clarifying or solving contemporary economic problems.

Although much of the course is patterned after the traditional principles course, there are at least six substantial differences.

First we study economic behavior and organization as one aspect of social behavior and organization; we study our 'economy' as a vital subsystem of U.S. and of world society. A major goal is for students to discover why economics is important—to discover the effects and functions of economic activity and organization in a society—to bring students somewhat closer to becoming economic determinists.

Second, the frame of reference we establish for studying the U.S. political economy is a general systems model of economic organization which describes the function of economic institutions in any society, the interdependence between economic and other social institutions and the relation between changes in institutional structure and economic development.

Third, and related to the previous point, students use the general theories about economic organization introduced in the course to study other types of economies—traditional American Indian tribes, underdeveloped economies and communist societies. These units permit students to clarify further their understanding of our own system by expanding their knowledge of other forms of economic organization.

Fourth, we make the course less abstract by de-emphasizing the expository teaching of economic theory. Students do not study economic "principles" in a vacuum as is usually the case; instead, they study those principles which describe or are exemplified by the economic behavior or institutional structure under investigation. We introduce only that traditional economic theory which provides an appropriate and efficient model of the markets or systems we include in the course.

Fifth, the course emphasizes analysis of economic conflicts and encourages students to take a stand or work toward a more reasoned opinion on controversial public policy issues. In this way we invite students to scrutinize or to start to develop their own economic ideology. Students apply economic theory and facts to study and make judgments about racism in the U.S. industry organization, poverty and trends in income distribution in the U.S., appropriate routes to and degrees of economic growth and stability for this economy, the prospects for development of poor countries and the prospects for development toward communist ideals in communist countries.

Finally, instead of emphasizing more-or-less rote learning of a standard portion of economic theory and public policy orthodoxy, we try to help students learn the abstract reasoning skills used by economists and economic philosophers. Ordinarily, principles instructors implicitly assume that students are already able to do abstract analysis, furthermore, that once they learn the principles of economics, they will automatically apply this kind of abstract reasoning to the solution of social problems. This is the justification for the standard teaching mode in which students read and listen to expositions of economic theory interspersed with applications of the theories to derive "appropriate" public policies for controlling prices, employment and output; farm prices and income; monopoly and labor unions; international money and output flows, etc. Students are fed both the theoretical principles and the policy orthodoxy which they are required to recognize or recall on examination. This forced feeding approach does not train students in the *process* of abstract reasoning; rather it requires them to memorize the *product* of the professions' abstracting. In contrast, to achieve ECON 12 objectives, students must learn economic reasoning processes. This requires them to construct models, to use models to explain or predict institutional or system behavior, to identify the issues involved in policy or ideological polemics, to synthesize their theoretical and factual knowledge into a defensible judgment.

## TEACHING STRATEGY

To permit students to learn economic reasoning skills, class and homework activities must be varied. In ECON 12 we make use of the standard kinds of instructional materials—text, programmed instruction, workbook exercises, readings, statistical abstract, overhead transparencies, and movies. However, they are constructed as parts of an integrated teaching system which permits the instructor to set up the variety of learning situations necessary to bring about student achievement of course objectives.

ECON 12 classes differ from ordinary introductory principles classes in the use of instructional modes which require active student participation in and responsibility for learning. Instead of relying on lectures and texts for didactic instruction, we substitute programmed instruction and a correlated, summary text, each designed to permit most students to learn a specified minimum body of knowledge and skills. We consider the programmed instruction format superior because it individualizes instruction by permitting students to work at their own speed, requiring them to participate by answering questions at the end of each frame, providing continual feedback and extra help, and restricting what is to be learned to a limited set of stated objectives. With less lecturing, more class time can be devoted to discussion and problem solving in which the total class or small groups of students work together to extend and apply the knowledge they have acquired in the programmed reading. Frequent written assignments give students further practice using the knowledge and skills and permit the instructor to judge the progress of individual students. Lectures, while less frequent, are used to introduce a new area of study, to tie together student ideas, to provide direction or additional ideas to facilitate student problem solving, and to summarize main ideas.

[The table entitled "Unit II: U.S. Market Systems" presents an analysis of the second part of this four-part course in economics.] (See following page.)

## UNIT II: THE U.S. MARKET SYSTEMS

| I. Theory | II. Analytic Framework for Analyzing Case Study Data or Readings | Case Studies | III. Inferences Drawn from the Comparison of Case Studies and Readings | IV. Ideological Issues |
|---|---|---|---|---|
| Cybernetics systems Use of line graphs Price determination using supply and demand curves Law of supply and demand Pure competition: long-run equilibrium conditions | Given five market structure characteristics, students predict: 1. Market conduct: pricing decisions, product decisions, changes in ownership; 2. Long-run industry performance | Industry studies: Aluminum, auto manufacture, telephone service | Theories about oligopoly conduct. Theories about oligopoly performance Generalizations about the impact of antitrust laws and public regulation | The nature of American capitalism, its effect on economic freedom, justice, security, progress, and stability |
| Demand elasticity Pure monopoly: long-run equilibrium conditions Classifying imperfectly competitive markets according to three market structure characteristics: market concentration, barriers to entry, product differentiation. | Given data on factors affecting income distribution in our market economy (government taxing and spending, wealth distribution, distribution of labor services) and factors affecting wage and salary differentials, students study the need for and impact of different government programs on different groups of the poor. | Poverty and public policy Government programs: Public assistance, negative income tax, public services, job opportunities, urban reform. | Generalizations about the effects of different government programs. Inferences about the kinds of programs necessary to eliminate poverty among various categories of the poor. Generalizations about the possibility of increasing the proportion of the labor force which is occupationally mobile. | The merits of guaranteeing equal opportunity and minimum living standards to all. |

Despite the innovative appeal of many new nontextbook materials and of courses capitalizing on a multimedia approach to teaching, recent texts for high school economics and problems courses show marked improvement over earlier books and are being widely adopted. In the last few years nearly a dozen high school economics texts, written by economists and educators with vast experience in economic education, have appeared. The authors have had considerable experience in teaching teachers and high school students and in consulting with school systems on the revision of curriculum. This classroom instructional experience has enhanced the value of their texts.

## Courses and Units Dependent on a K-11 Sequence

So far our attention has been directed to economics courses and study units that do not presuppose earlier encounters with economics. This section contains suggestions for the capstone course or the final unit in a curriculum sequence built on earlier study of economics. We begin by quoting four paragraphs of rationale adapted from an unpublished curriculum document by Bruce Johnstone of the Minnesota Center for Economic Education:

### THE CONTENT OF THE CAPSTONE COURSE

The most common weakness of the capstone course is probably the over-extension of course content into all applied areas traditionally encompassed within the typical college course in economics principles. There seems to be a tacit conviction that any course which is called "economics" must teach distinct units on the stock market, labor unions, world trade, conservation, and—only at the end of the course —comparative economic systems (which often accords equal time to fascism, and only grudgingly admits to varieties of socialism).

All of these topics, of course, are valuable, both for the practical relevance of their content and in the practice they provide for the exercise of that perspective which emerges from the structure of the discipline. None of them, however, is an indispensable ingredient in the establishment of that structure or perspective. They should be chosen, then—and chosen selectively—either because they are important in themselves, or because they illustrate and provide practice in the application of the perspective and method of economics. They should not be included out of a mistaken notion that they are economics, or that economics need be something less without them.

The misallocation of content coverage was noted in the 1962 report of the Textbooks Study Committee of the American Economic Association. The report cited a notable over-emphasis on consumer problems, the stock market, and conservation and a frequent under-emphasis on the cultural basis of an economic system, reconciliation of the theoretical and the actual behavior of the firm, the nature of economic controversy, and the principles of welfare economics.

The rationale for teaching "directly to" economics at some point, rather than relying on other course and subject contexts is the conviction that economics is a highly structured discipline which must at some point be seen in its entirety. The "individual pieces"—the concepts and generalizations—can be taught in a great many contexts. The perspective of the economist, however, comes only when these pieces are put together into a whole which is then something more than the sum of the pieces.

In putting these individual pieces together teachers and other curriculum developers throughout the country have relied heavily on the basic kind of organization mentioned in Part One of this book. An overview of the activities selected for Part Two shows that there is a unity of curriculum content in grades K through 11. The economic strands which are woven through these grades join to make up the core of the twelfth-grade course. The objective of the twelfth-grade course for students who already have some economic understandings is to reinforce previous learning, to complete learning vital to basic economic analysis, and to provide practice in viewing social phenomena from the porch of economics.

The guide for the first two objectives has been previously illustrated in grades K through 11. If there were perfect learning and retention, there would be no need for including these two objectives in the twelfth grade.

To provide practice in finding interrelationships in economic activities we describe three ways in which a culminating course might achieve greater depth in presenting the economic perspective. Before doing so, however, it is a good idea to repeat a few points made earlier.

No matter how we define capstone course, the fact is that elements from such a course may be meaningful in any course or unit in economics. No sacred aura is attached to the term capstone. Conversely, instructional modules from courses not considered capstone may be ideal for capstone courses.

Three ways in which the course may be enriched are the use of games and simulations, the use of mathematical models, and the use of accounting and statistics.

## Games and Simulations

Greater reliance is currently being placed on the use of games and simulations to advance learning because gaming and simulating situations permit the student to partake of many of the elements that typify real world situations. There are the added advantages of more immediate payoff and also stimulation from competition.

Two games are cited here as illustrative of the general field. They have been chosen because they have been in use for a number of years and their qualities have been demonstrated. First is the market game originally developed by Professor Myron L. Joseph of Carnegie-Mellon University. This game is part of the *Economics Reading for Students of Ninth Grade Social Studies,* Pittsburgh Public Schools. Its simplicity plus the fact that it requires no special equipment makes it especially commendable. In essence, different members of a class are designated as buyers or sellers of a commodity, for example, wheat. By having students make bids for the commodity in an auctionlike situation, there is a demonstration of the concepts of supply and demand and finally of the general notion of market equilibrium. The excitement and enthusiasm of participants together with their learning of essential economic principles has made it attractive to students and teachers.

Another more complicated game was developed by Professor Ralph N. Calkins of Hanover College, Indiana.* Although the game was designed for the college course in principles of economics, it could be adapted for high school use. (Calkins makes use of the computer to handle the participants' decisions but the computer is not essential.)

Calkins' model includes a group of firms in the chewing-gum industry. Each student is the manager of a firm in this industry. He has the choice of investing his allotted sum of money either in producing gum, in the raw materials, or in the securities of materials' suppliers. The demand for the product is fixed and given. The entrepreneurs' activities therefore consist essentially of supplying the commodity to market while attempting to maximize their profits. Through their

*"A Computerized Model of Exchange as an Aid to Teaching Price Theory," *Journal of Economic Education,* Spring 1970.

competition for materials, they drive up the prices of the ingredients of manufacture. After a series of decisions among the entrepreneurs about the investments they will make, students learn about rising cost curves and the effect of competition thereon.

## Mathematical Models

Although there is danger to both teaching and learning economics by excessive stress on mathematical manipulation, it is nevertheless true that for certain students and in certain schools in which more is done with mathematics, opportunities abound for the mathematical treatment of economic science. The games and simulations often include the construction of a model with specific mathematical properties. The examination of these properties can explain both the economics and the mathematics in an interesting manner.

The field of macroeconomics is especially suited to the development of a wide spectrum of mathematical models. The circular flow notion can be expressed in a highly simplified three-equation model of the Keynesian variety; for example, the idea that national income $(Y)$ is the sum of business investment $(I)$ and consumer spending $(C)$ (neglecting government and foreign spending) may be expressed as

$$Y = C + I$$

The idea of the consumption function in which consumption is related to some level of income may be expressed as

$$C = a + bY$$

To illustrate the interpretation of this relationship: If the constants $a$ and $b$ are assumed to have values of 100 and 0.8, respectively, the expression $C = a + bY$ becomes $C = 100 + 0.8Y$, meaning that consumer spending is 100 plus eight-tenths the level of income. Now, if income $Y$ is 600, the equation is solved as follows:

$$C = 100 + (0.8 \times 600) = 100 + 480 = 580$$

If the level of investment is assumed to be known (or for that matter the value of any of the variables) a simple model like this can be used to arrive at the level of national income. As economists know, one can go from this brief exposition into as great a complexity as seems suitable, including such matters as government spending and net foreign investment, on the demand side, and on the outgo side such elements as transfer payments by government and tax relationships.

138

A third and final way in which depth may be given to twelfth-grade instruction involves accounting and statistics. The leading systems of accounts include national income accounts, business income accounts, balance of payments accounts, interindustry accounts, and money-flows accounts. Through the use of any accounting system, one kind of quantified perspective on economic activity may be given. Except to a few students in business courses, this view will not have been presented during their elementary and high school years. Therefore this presents an opportunity to give a scientific, rigorous, and quantified presentation of economic activity and the exact definition to such ideas as profit, loss, assets, and liabilities. A variety of other accounting concepts may be illustrated.

Just as accounting provides the categories into which various economic measurements may be placed to illustrate relationships, statistics also provide measures of the degree of accuracy that may be attributed to these magnitudes. It is one thing to know that profits of an economic activity are $1,287,542.22; it is quite another matter to determine that this figure is subject to an error of plus or minus $450,000.

The science of statistics lends degrees of credibility to most numerical measures. To illustrate: If the cost of living goes up, as measured by the Consumer Price Index of the Bureau of Labor Statistics, it is relevant to have some understanding of the accuracy of this measure. Similar stipulations apply to most economic measures, including unemployment, poverty, national income, and wages.

Some teachers may wish to stress the use of statistics in testing hypotheses; for example, imagine that students in a class visit two different stores and compare prices on a list of two dozen identical items. If they find that the average of prices in one store is 10 cents higher than the average in the other store, what is the probability that this result is merely due to sampling error and not to any real difference in average prices between the stores? In testing the hypothesis that there is a real difference of 10 cents between the average prices of the two stores, just how reliable the sample of prices is matters a great deal.

Students who have watched election returns on television in which samples of votes throughout a state or region are used to forecast election results will readily take to the notion that the same method of statistical sampling is applicable to their own work. This application may serve to enliven discussion and enrich learning.

Capable twelfth graders should become acquainted with some of the leading sources of information on the economy. The following government publications should be helpful.

*Economic Report of the President*

Each January the President and his economic advisers issue a summary of recent economic activity, discussions of fiscal and monetary policy, and a forecast of prospects ahead. The report contains extensive numerical data on income, prices, wages, and federal finance. Originator: Council of Economic Advisers, Executive Office Building, Washington, D.C. 20506.

*Historical Statistics of the United States: Colonial Times to 1957*

A vast collection of historical statistics which has been updated by *Continuation to 1962 and Revisions.* Originator: United States Department of Commerce, Bureau of the Census, Washington, D.C.20230.

*Report on the President's Economic Report.*

After the President has issued his report, a joint committee of the House and Senate gives its response, often with lively dissents from minority members. Originator: Joint Economic Committee, United States Congress, Washington, D.C. 20510. Many other valuable studies are originated by the Committee which publishes a listing of available reports.

The following monthly periodicals may be ordered from the publishing government agency or the Superintendent of Documents, United States Government Printing Office, Washington, D.C. 20402.

*Federal Reserve Bulletin.*

This journal is crammed with monetary data. It discusses policy and related matters. Board of Governors of the Federal Reserve System, Washington, D.C. 20551.

*Monthly Labor Review.*

This review does for the area of labor (wages, trade unionism, etc.) what the Federal Reserve Bulletin cited above does for money matters.

United States Department of Labor, Bureau of Labor Statistics, Washington, D.C. 20212.

*Survey of Current Business*

This monthly publication of the U.S. Department of Commerce provides detailed statistics on all aspects of the American economy as well as analytical articles on such matters as the GNP, the balance of payments, industrial production, and state and local finance. United States Department of Commerce, Office of Business Economics, Washington, D.C. 20230.

# Selected Bibliography of Teaching and Learning Materials*

These classroom materials for teachers and students were prepared by cooperating schools in the Developmental Economic Education Program (DEEP).

## Elementary

*ECONOMICS IN THE ELEMENTARY SCHOOL: WHY, WHAT, WHERE? A Handbook for Teachers.* Minneapolis: Minneapolis Public Schools, 1967.
> Outlines the need for economic education, summarizes content appropriate for elementary schools, and offers suggestions for economic emphasis at each grade level.

*ECONOMIC EDUCATION, A Supplement to the Social Studies Guide, Kindergarten, First Grade, Second Grade.* Minneapolis: Minneapolis Public Schools, 1967.
> The first in a K-12 series. By grouping the primary level guides into this one volume, the supplements can help teachers plan for continuity of concept development across grade levels. Includes suggested teaching-learning activities and resources. The context for concept development is the home, school and neighborhood.

*ECONOMIC EDUCATION, A Supplement to the Social Studies Guide, Third Grade, Fourth Grade.* Minneapolis: Minneapolis Public Schools, 1967.
> Economic concepts, producer, consumer, and factors of production, are identified; suggested teaching-learning activities provide the teacher with a strategy for instruction.

*GOODS, SERVICES, AND PEOPLE, An Economics Sequence for the Primary Grades.* Des Moines, Iowa: Des Moines Public Schools, 1967.
> A supplement for the social studies guides for kindergarten through third grade. Provides teachers with a nontechnical overview of six basic economic concepts to be taught; outlines step-by-step grade-level development of basic concepts; gives examples and activities illustrating ways to present basic concepts.

*Available from the Joint Council on Economic Education, 1212 Avenue of the Americas, New York, New York 10036.

*ECONOMIC EDUCATION FOR WASHINGTON SCHOOLS, Kindergarten through Grade Six.* Olympia, Washington: Washington State Department of Public Instruction, 1966.

There is a common format for the guidelines in which concepts are presented and developed in terms of student interpretations. Supplementary activities and a bibliography are provided at the end of each grade section. Each new concept has an explanatory note to the teacher.

*TEACHERS GUIDE TO ECONOMICS, GRADE 1.* Salem, Oregon: Oregon State Department of Public Instruction, 1968.
*TEACHERS GUIDE TO ECONOMICS, GRADE 2.* Salem, Oregon: Oregon State Department of Public Instruction, 1968.
*TEACHERS GUIDE TO ECONOMICS, GRADE 3.* Salem, Oregon: Oregon State Department of Public Instruction, 1968.
*TEACHERS GUIDE TO ECONOMICS, GRADE 4.* Salem, Oregon: Oregon State Department of Public Instruction, 1968.
*TEACHERS GUIDE TO ECONOMICS, GRADE 5.* Salem, Oregon: Oregon State Department of Public Instruction, 1968.
*TEACHERS GUIDE TO ECONOMICS, GRADE 8.* Salem, Oregon: Oregon State Department of Public Instruction, 1968.

The Oregon series of social studies supplements, which identifies basic economic concepts appropriate to the particular grade, provides teaching activities and lists of resources, and gives suggestions for evaluating student understanding of the material.

## Junior High School

*ECONOMIC EDUCATION FOR WASHINGTON SCHOOLS, Grades Seven, Eight and Nine.* Olympia, Washington: Washington State Department of Public Instruction, 1967.

This volume continues the grade sequence and economic themes begun in the Washington K-6 program. Economic concepts in grade seven center on the geography of Western Europe, the Soviet Union, and Sub-Sahara Africa; in grade eight they center around a course in American history; and in grade nine around a course in Washington State history.

*MINNEAPOLIS TRADES WITH JAPAN, A Supplement to Grade 7 Geography.* Minneapolis: Minneapolis Public Schools, 1967.

Deals with the mechanics and theory of international trade, development problems of eastern hemisphere countries, and the growth of Japan's economy.

*U.S. ECONOMIC GROWTH TO 1865, A Supplement for Grade 8 American History.* Minneapolis: Minneapolis Public Schools, 1967.

> Contains seven lessons to be inserted in the history curriculum; capital formation, improved technology, westward expansion, government policy, railroad expansion, labor supply, and money supply.

*ECONOMICS READINGS FOR STUDENTS OF EIGHTH-GRADE UNITED STATES HISTORY and TEACHER'S MANUAL.* Pittsburgh: Pittsburgh Public Schools, 1966.

> Economic growth is the main theme, with emphasis on economic concepts as analytical tools to help understand historical events. Teacher's manual explains the economic concepts developed and suggests use with students of varying abilities and background. Lesson plans include clearly stated objectives. There are sketches suitable for transparencies, appropriate test questions, and background information helpful to the teacher.

*ECONOMICS READINGS FOR STUDENTS OF NINTH-GRADE SOCIAL SCIENCE and TEACHER'S MANUAL.* Pittsburgh: Pittsburgh Public Schools, 1967.

> Complements and expands the concepts stressed in the eighth-grade materials including economic scarcity, real cost, and productive resources. Students are given a real-life situation to analyze which requires use of the economic ideas taught through the readings.

*THE ECONOMICS OF POVERTY and TEACHER'S MANUAL.* Pittsburgh: Pittsburgh Public Schools, 1968.

> This problem-solving unit is suitable for supplementary reading in any high school economics or social-studies course. Economic analysis is applied in nontechnical language to the problem of poverty. Many agencies enlisted in antipoverty efforts are discussed; case study material is used. Teacher's manual provides 13 lesson plans which outline objectives, and include information to help the teacher field student questions.

*MANPOWER AND ECONOMIC EDUCATION: OPPORTUNITIES IN AMERICAN ECONOMIC LIFE and TEACHER MANUAL.* Columbus, Ohio: Ohio University Center for Economic Education, 1968.

> This 75-lesson course, field-tested in the eighth, ninth, and tenth grades in eight Ohio schools, describes how students can enhance their employability by investing in the development of knowledge, skills, motivation, and behavior patterns. Lessons include case histories and questions to be answered in classroom discussions or in writing. Statistical data are provided to develop "statistical literacy."

# Senior High School

*THE ECONOMIC EFFECTS OF EDUCATION, A Supplement for Secondary School Social Studies.* Minneapolis: Minneapolis Public Schools, 1967.

A resource for any secondary course. Education as an investment is emphasized and how it benefits the student and the nation. Tabular data and bibliography are provided.

*THE INDUSTRIAL REVOLUTION, A Supplement for Grade 10 World History.* Minneapolis: Minneapolis Public Schools, 1967.

Deals with economic growth and development in market-oriented societies and highlights episodes in the economic development of Europe, notably Great Britain.

*READINGS IN ECONOMICS FOR 10th GRADE STUDENTS OF WORLD CULTURES and TEACHER'S MANUAL.* Pittsburgh: Pittsburgh Public Schools, 1967.

An introduction to the economics of world trade, related problems and some solutions. Graphs and tables list American imports and exports from colonial times to the present. Analytical tools to analyze world trade problems are also described. Readings define, in simple terms, current issues related to balance of payments, tariffs, and international monetary systems, and stress interdependence between nations.

*ECONOMIC EXPANSION IN THE UNITED STATES SINCE 1865, A Supplement for Grade 11 U.S. History.* Minneapolis: Minneapolis Public Schools, 1967.

This supplement for teachers explains the major elements in economic growth since the Civil War. The material can be used at different times during the eleventh-grade U.S. history course.

*THE COMING OF THE GREAT DEPRESSION, A Supplement to Grade 11 U.S. History.* Minneapolis: Minneapolis Public Schools, 1967.

Focuses on the imbalances in spending and production decisions, the misallocation of resources, and the changes in public optimism leading to the depression in the 1930's. Charts, tables, and a bibliography are included.

*READINGS IN ECONOMICS FOR 11th GRADE STUDENTS OF UNITED STATES HISTORY, A UNIT ON THE GREAT DEPRESSION and TEACHER'S MANUAL.* Pittsburgh: Pittsburgh Public Schools, 1968.

A case study of how the 1930's depression affected Pittsburgh. Readings reflect the successive efforts by the private sector and city, state, and federal governments to help the jobless. Many tables and graphs are included for analyzing the results of these efforts to stabilize Pittsburgh's depressed economy.

*READINGS IN ECONOMICS FOR 12th GRADE STUDENTS OF AMERICAN DEMOCRACY and TEACHER'S MANUAL.* Pittsburgh: Pittsburgh Public Schools, 1968.

A 12-week course covering economic principles as applied to economic problems. Focuses on the development, operation, and problems of a market economy but also contains readings about comparative economic systems including that of the U.S.S.R. Designed to help students develop a rational approach to problem solving and also a healthy scepticism in their own thinking.

*A RESOURCE DOCUMENT FOR A HIGH SCHOOL COURSE IN THE UNITED STATES ECONOMY.* Sacramento: California State Department of Education, 1967.

Focuses on organizing and outlining the essential content of a high school economics course. Provides guidelines and information that curriculum specialists and teachers can use in developing their own course outlines, instructional guides, and materials on various aspects of economics.

*ECONOMIC EDUCATION FOR WASHINGTON SCHOOLS, Grades Ten, Eleven and Twelve.* Olympia, Washington: Washington State Department of Public Instruction, 1968.

This volume continues the grade sequence and economic themes of the Washington K-9 program. Grade-ten course includes economic history and the economics of Western Europe, the United States, the Soviet Union, and Latin America. Grade-eleven material centers on American history from 1607 to 1945. Grade-twelve material suggests two capstone courses: a recapitulation of economic concepts or an American problems course.

## Tests

*TEST OF ECONOMIC UNDERSTANDING.* Chicago: Science Research Associates, 1968.

Instrument to assess student understanding of the basic economic concepts deemed essential by the National Task Force on Economic Education.

*TEST OF UNDERSTANDING IN COLLEGE ECONOMICS.* New York: The Psychological Corporation, 1968.

Available in two parts, part one, macroeconomics; part two, microeconomics. To preserve the integrity of *TUCE* the distribution is restricted to educational institutions.

# *Economic Education in the Schools*

A REPORT OF THE
NATIONAL TASK FORCE
ON ECONOMIC EDUCATION

# Members of the Task Force

GEORGE LELAND BACH, CHAIRMAN
*Dean, Graduate School of*
*Industrial Administration*
*Carnegie Institute of Technology*

ARNO A. BELLACK
*Professor of Education, Teachers College*
*Columbia University*

LESTER V. CHANDLER
*Chairman, Department of Economics*
*Princeton University*

M. L. FRANKEL
*Director*
*Joint Council on Economic Education*

ROBERT AARON GORDON
*Chairman, Department of Economics*
*University of California, Berkeley*

BEN W. LEWIS
*Chairman, Department of Economics*
*Oberlin College*

PAUL A. SAMUELSON
*Professor of Economics*
*Massachusetts Institute of Technology*

FLOYD A. BOND, Executive Secretary
*Dean, School of Business Administration*
*University of Michigan*

# Contents

# *Preface*

In July, 1960, we were pleased to announce creation of a National Task Force on Economic Education, composed of five of the nation's outstanding economists and two of its leading secondary school educators. The primary mission of the Task Force was to describe the minimum understanding of economics essential for good citizenship and attainable by high school students, with the goal of providing helpful guidelines for high school teachers, administrators, and school boards.

This National Task Force, unique in the history of American economics, was announced jointly by the American Economic Association (the professional association of America's economists, totalling some 10,000 in number), which appointed the members of the Task Force, and the Committee for Economic Development, which offered to finance the study. Once created, however, the Task Force became completely independent of the two organizations. Its findings are subject to review by no agency or organization, nor is either of the sponsoring organizations responsible for the findings. Every precaution has been taken to establish a group of unquestioned objectivity and to protect it from any trace of pressures from particular interest groups in our economy.

The Task Force is a distinguished one. Its economist members, at the time of appointment, included the president-elect of the American Economic Association, its two vice-presidents, a member of its executive committee, and the chairman of its Committee on Economic Education. All five are distinguished authors and teachers. The two members from the field of education are similarly experienced in the teaching of economics and social studies at the high school level. In its work the Task Force has drawn on the advice of many additional experts from the fields of economics and education.

This report represents the findings of the Task Force after a year of hard and careful work. We commend it to everyone interested in the economic literacy of our youth—to school boards, school administrators and teachers, and to the general public, on whose support the standards in our schools must ultimately depend. Its first chapter paints a disturbing picture of the absence of the teaching of economics in high schools, the only place where we can be sure of reaching most of the citizens of tomorrow. For less than half of all high school graduates go on to college, and only about a quarter of these ever take a college course in economics. Chapters II and III spell out in detail an admirably well-rounded and objective picture of the kind of economic understanding needed for responsible citizenship and effective participation in today's complex economy. In Chapter IV the Task Force presents concrete recommendations for steps to improve the level of economic understanding developed in our schools.

Those seeking to forward special interests and those who believe that the teaching of economics should be indoctrination will find scant comfort in the report. For it stresses, above all, the development of objective, reasoned consideration of economic issues as a basis for thorough understanding and wise choice. Its spirit is the spirit of working democracy. We believe this is as it should be.

DONALD K. DAVID
*Chairman, Committee for Economic Development*

THEODORE W. SCHULTZ
*President, American Economic Association 1960*

# ONE

## *The Need for Economic Education*

ECONOMIC UNDERSTANDING is essential if we are to meet our responsibilities as citizens and as participants in a basically private enterprise economy. Many of the most important issues in government policy are economic in nature, and we face economic problems at every turn in our day-to-day lives. Consider, for example, some of the economic issues confronting the nation and many of us as individuals in recent years: inflation, recession and unemployment, a lagging rate of economic growth, the impact of automation, the "farm problem," financing of schools and highways, medical care for the aged, foreign aid, government deficits, and taxes. Economic problems arise at every level—national, state, and local—and in both public and private affairs.

The economic role of government and the complexity of the economic issues with which it deals have grown enormously in the past fifty years. For this there have been many reasons—the increase and urbanization of our population, the sheer growth of wealth and incomes, rapid scientific and technological change, two world wars, a great depression, continuing international tensions, and changing attitudes toward government. One may approve or deplore the power of government in economic affairs, but no one can deny its existence nor that the quality of government policies is a major force in determining the performance of our entire economic system.

In the final analysis, the effectiveness of government depends on the capacity and understanding of the people. For it is the people who, through their votes and other influences, determine within broad limits the scope and nature of government policies. If they are to exercise their great political power responsibly and effectively, more of our people must know more about our economy and must learn to think about economic issues objectively and rationally. The alternative is to make decisions on the basis of ignorance and prejudice. Nor is the case for economic understanding limited to preparation for effective voting. Leaders in every walk of life—business, labor, agriculture—

155

need to understand the American economy, as do the people who work for the businesses and who are the members of the unions.

If our citizens of tomorrow are to achieve the desired minimum economic understanding, most of them must get it in the schools. It is no good to say that they can wait until college, for less than half of them go on to college, and most of those do not study economics when they get there. Thus, most of our youth must rely on the high schools for the economics they are to learn.

## How Are the Schools Meeting Their Responsibility for Developing Economic Understanding?

The understanding of the American economy developed in most high schools today is not adequate for effective citizenship. While excellent teaching of economics occurs in some schools, very few high school students take a course in economics; textbooks and other teaching materials are all too often inadequate; and most teachers in the social studies have insufficient preparation in economics to teach the subject effectively. Despite a trend in recent years toward inclusion of more economics in the schools, the existing situation is far from satisfactory.

*Economics in the Curriculum*

Apparently only about five per cent of all high school students ever take a separate course in economics. Perhaps half of all high school students do study "Problems of American Democracy," or a similarly oriented "problems" course, in which a substantial block of time is devoted to economic aspects of current broad social problems, such as natural resources, labor-management relations, and social security. Nearly all students take a course in American history, where some attention is given to the development of economic institutions and legislation. Scattered attention is given to economic institutions and problems at a variety of other points in the curriculum, notably in the social studies courses throughout the grades.

Even in the separate course in economics, however, the orientation is generally descriptive and all too often dry and sterile. Little attention is given to helping students learn to think for themselves about the big economic problems our nation faces today. Few analytical concepts are developed, and fewer are used. In the problems of American democracy and American history courses, even less attention is given

156

to the development of independent analytical thinking by students on economic problems. The flavor of these courses is often chronological and descriptive, with teachers placing primary stress on those areas where their own training is strongest, usually in history. On economic issues it appears that teachers often insert their own value judgments and "answers" on economic issues as to what the student should believe, all too often without identifying them as such.

### Teaching Materials

Teaching materials are improving, but they remain generally inadequate. A recent survey of the economics content of leading textbooks for courses in economics, problems of American democracy, and American history, made by three groups of respected American economists, indicates that high school students are being given a running glance at a wide array of economic topics, but that only in rare cases are the teaching materials focused on developing fundamental economic understanding.

The treatment in textbooks is mainly descriptive; economic analysis is almost entirely absent; the reasoning is often loose and superficial; value judgments of the authors, generally unidentified as such, abound. The committees reported that these books generally fail to develop an awareness of what the fundamental economic problems are, and of how rational, objective reasoning can contribute effectively to their solution. In the American history books, to which most high school students are exposed, the treatment of economics is primarily descriptive and fails to emphasize economic analysis of the major problems involved, since the emphasis of the books is historical.

Since most social studies teachers have had little, if any, formal training in economics, they cannot reasonably be expected to add to their textbooks an objective, analytical approach to the understanding of the modern American economy. The quality of textbooks and other teaching materials thus becomes all the more important.

In addition to textbooks, there is a mass of special pamphlets and materials available to social studies teachers in the high schools. These materials, flooding the schools, come from institutions and organizations of every description, many of them with propaganda intent. Some of these publications represent sound scholarship and a genuine desire to make available objective and useful information. Since most teachers are neither adequately prepared nor have the time to assess all of this printed matter, its usefulness in most high school teaching is dubious. The large volume of urgent requests from teachers and administrators for evaluation of such publications, and for lists of recommended books, pamphlets and audiovisual aids, reveals the desperate need for assistance felt by those responsible for teaching economics in the high schools.

## The Teachers

Today we rely primarily on high school teachers in the social studies and American history to develop understanding of the American economy. While most of these teachers are conscientious and sincere, only a little more than half of them have ever had as much as a single college course in economics to prepare them for this important part of their teaching job. Most of these have apparently had only one or two college courses in economics. Virtually none have undergraduate majors in economics, even those teaching special courses in economics in the high schools.

Obviously, teachers who have inadequate preparation cannot be expected to do an adequate job in the classroom. This explains why economic analysis gets virtually no attention in most history courses, and is often poorly taught in problems of American democracy and civics courses. To make this point is not to malign the training, skill, and splendid work of many able and dedicated teachers in the high schools. It is merely to be realistic about the necessity of adequate training to do a proper job.

State teacher certification requirements are intended to provide minimum standards for teachers. Yet apparently only sixteen of the fifty states require even an elementary course in economics for certification to teach high school social studies. This situation is reflected in the curricula of the colleges that train teachers in the social studies. In a recent study of social studies teacher programs in fifty selected colleges and universities throughout the country, thirty-eight were found to offer a major in social studies. Of these, only twenty-five required any economics for the major, with a median requirement of only one year of elementary economics for these teachers of tomorrow who will be largely responsible for teaching basic understanding of the American economy in our schools.

The dearth of teachers able to teach economics was dramatically illustrated recently when a large city decided to introduce economics into its high schools. The operation would have required 300 teachers, but only seventeen could be found with adequate training for the task!

## The Public's Attitude

Recently, there has been a strong growth of interest in the teaching of economics in the high schools. Only with such basic public support can real improvement in this area come about. Unfortunately, it is necessary to recognize that many individuals and groups see economics in the schools as a device for stressing their own viewpoints, as an opportunity to foist on the schools their own private views. Too many do not recognize the value of impartial analysis and discussion of varying viewpoints and interpretations of controversial issues. Too many insist, indeed, that controversial issues should be avoided in the classroom. Most important problems are controversial, and today large numbers of social studies teachers avoid controversial issues because they fear public criticism. This is not the way to train our youth to face the important problems that will confront them as citizens. It is not the way to the development of sound economic understanding.

## Summary

In summary, although there are many spots of excellence, most of the high schools are not developing in our youth today the understanding of the American economy that they must have to meet effectively their responsibilities as citizens. We believe that positive steps can and should be taken to improve this situation. In Chapters II and III we describe the minimum amount of economic understanding which we recommend as essential for effective citizenship. Chapter IV presents our recommendations and suggestions for steps toward achieving this understanding.

# TWO

---

## *The Need for a Rational Approach to Economic Problems*

*Why Economic Understanding Is Important*

As we have seen, modern man is faced with a host of economic problems. This is the basic reason why economic understanding is important. Such personal decisions as what occupation to enter, how to spend his income, or in what form to invest his savings, he must be prepared to answer himself.

Others are public economic problems at the state and local level on which he must decide and vote as a citizen. Should he, for example, vote to raise taxes in his community to finance better schools, or to bring new industries into his region? Should the state's unemployment compensation law provide larger and longer benefits?

Still others face us at the national level, such as what the federal government should do to support high employment and rapid growth while at the same time preventing inflationary increases in prices? If a recession threatens, what steps can and should be taken? Indeed, why do we have recurring periods of boom and slack times?

Americans live and work in a particular kind of economic system. Many people call it a "private enterprise" system. What are the essential characteristics of this system, and how does it differ from others? How do consumers make their wishes known so that the goods they want are produced in the right quantities? What role does competition play, and what sort of antimonopoly legislation do we need? Why does agriculture (the most competitive of all our industries) seem to be in continuous trouble, and hence, what should we do about the "farm problem"?

On the international level, should we have tariffs to protect domestic markets for American producers? How much foreign aid can, and should we afford for the underdeveloped nations?

All these questions—and many others—must be answered. We can

160

answer them on the basis of ignorance and emotion, or we can act *rationally;* that is, on the basis of a reasonable understanding of how the economy operates, a clear recognition of the goals we want to achieve, an appraisal of the relevant facts, and a reasoned choice of that line of action which will best achieve our goals. Everyone must to some extent act as his own economist—in his private life and as a citizen—and both he and the community will be better served if he is well informed and can think clearly and objectively about economic questions.

What we want to emphasize is the need to develop in the student the ability to reason clearly and objectively about economic issues. The future citizen needs to acquire a modest amount of factual information about the economic world, but the primary obligation of the schools is to help him to develop his capacity to think clearly, objectively, and with a reasonable degree of sophistication about economic problems. Mere description of economic institutions is not what we mean by economic education.

In this connection, we believe that training in economic analysis does more than just contribute to the student's understanding of how our economic system operates. As we emphasize repeatedly in these pages, the development of economic understanding involves first and above all the capacity to think *rationally* about economic issues. In this respect, the teaching of economics can make an important contribution to the student's mental development. It is in the field of the social sciences—with respect to social, political, and economic questions—that the high school graduate's ability to reason clearly and objectively is probably weakest.

## A Rational Way of Thinking About Economic Problems

*The most important step toward understanding in economics—as in other branches of knowledge—is the replacement of emotional, unreasoned judgments by objective, rational analysis. This is the first lesson to be learned in approaching the study of economics.* Above all else, economic education should emphasize that rational, objective analysis is needed on economic issues, large and small. Such analysis of problems will not necessarily bring agreement. But it will greatly lessen the reliance on prejudice, emotion, and name-calling that unfortunately dominates so much popular discussion of economic problems.

In economics itself, the central problem is economizing—making the best use of the scarce productive resources available to us to satisfy our many wants. For resources to satisfy our wants are limited in amount and therefore are not free for the asking. Hence we must *choose* among the possible alternative uses to which these scarce resources can be put—whether to save or to spend, whether to spend our incomes on one object or on another, whether to tax ourselves more in order to finance government services, or to tax less and leave more for private spending. One of the essential lessons of economics is that we cannot have our cake and eat it too.

Given this overriding element of scarcity, the core of most economic issues is the need to make intelligent choices among competing alternatives. This process of choosing among alternatives does not always involve, directly and obviously, the problem of coping with the fact of scarcity. But indirectly and ultimately the problem is always there. It is the essence of economics that we have to think and plan and work to make what we have go as far as possible toward satisfying the objectives we consider most important.

Rational choice, whether we are dealing with economic or other kinds of problems, involves at least four stages:

*First,* we must define the problem. What are the facts? What issues are raised? Where are we in relation to where we want to go?

*Second,* we must identify our goals or objectives and give them some rough order of priority.

*Third,* we must look for the principal alternative ways of attaining these objectives—given the limited resources available to us and the other restrictions that may be imposed on our freedom of action. This gives us the alternatives from which we must make a choice.

*Fourth,* we must analyze the consequences of choosing each possible line of action. The course of action which, on the basis of such analysis, contributes most to our most important goals is clearly the "best" answer.

These are nothing more than the stages in a sound businessman's thinking as he makes an important decision. To take a noneconomic example, they are the same steps that a good scientist or physician follows in his work. A wise government goes through much the same steps when it determines economic policies. The same kind of orderly thinking also underlies rational economic choice for individuals and families.

The second of these four stages in orderly thinking calls for particular comment at this point. In solving any economic problem, we need to clarify the goals we want to obtain.

A good deal of economic misunderstanding would disappear if people always recognized clearly and made explicit the goals that they consider most important. Few people choose their most important private and social goals on the basis of economic reasoning alone. These goals are largely matters of basic belief that cannot themselves be proved or disproved by the laws of logic or by appeal to facts. For example, some people may consider individual economic freedom most important, others security, and still others what they regard as an equitable distribution of income. But however determined, it is essential that basic goals be clearly recognized—both personal goals and the broader social objectives.

To give a specific example, most Americans today agree on such general goals as higher living standards, maximum economic freedom for the individual, and less inequality of opportunity. On the other hand, a Russian could hardly be expected to agree with our views about the advantages of permitting consumers' demands to direct what should be produced, for his value judgments give little weight to the desirability of individuals being free to make their own spending and saving decisions.

Logical argument requires a clear statement of the assumptions from which we start. Similarly, clear thinking on economic matters requires recognition of goals that we take for granted—and that we also recognize how others may take for granted goals unlike our own. Thus, the clear recognition that differences in goals do exist within our own society should make a significant contribution to a fundamental aspect of democracy—respect for and tolerance of differences in opinion, and an understanding of how such differences may arise.

The many heated arguments about tariffs provide a good illustration of competing and contradictory goals. To employers and workers in an industry threatened by foreign competition, personal goals are likely to be paramount. Workers want most of all to keep their jobs, businessmen to hold their markets. But consumers, on the other hand, may want foreign competition to force down prices. Which goal shall have top priority? Clearly, how we evaluate a new tariff may be different depending on which set of goals we accept.

Let us now see how all the four stages in orderly economic thinking indicated above can contribute to intelligent decisions on a debated economic issue. Consider, for example, the question of what, if anything, we should do to control inflation.

First, we need to define the problem and resolve it into its elements. What are the facts? How much have various prices and costs been rising? Are there pressures toward further rises? What have been the most important results of inflation in the past?

Second, what goals are we trying to achieve? Is it most important to insure that continued inflation does not lead to a serious depression? Or is our chief aim to protect the creditors, bondholders and widows on pensions who will be paid in dollars of decreasing purchasing power if inflation continues? How important is it to achieve the highest attainable rate of economic growth, despite possible inflationary consequences? And what is our attitude toward direct government restrictions on individual economic freedom as, for example, through price and wage controls? These goals need to be weighed and ranked in importance.

The third step is to lay out the alternative courses of action available and to consider the consequences of each in terms of our objectives. We may tentatively decide that the chief alternatives are (1) cut down on the public's spending power by raising taxes, (2) force the banks to reduce the amount of credit they extend to business and consumers, (3) pass legislation imposing ceilings on wages and prices, or (4) do nothing beyond what is now being done.

A grasp of economic concepts and institutions is needed to evaluate these alternatives. We need only mention some possible conclusions here. One might find for example, that restriction of total private spending is the central need, and therefore favor alternatives 1 and 2. Or we might conclude that restriction of total spending will seriously slow down the rate of economic growth. Again, we may decide that the current inflation arises largely from the upward push of wages and special groups of industrial prices, which restriction of total private spending would not restrain effectively. This might lead us toward alternative 3. But we may hesitate to choose that path because it so obviously and directly interferes with free markets and free collective bargaining. Perhaps the analysis will suggest other alternatives that seem more satisfactory in terms of our objectives.

The fourth and final step is to decide what action is best, all things considered. This decision is often not easy. We may not be able to achieve all our goals, and choosing among them is painful. We may not be sure just what results will follow from the alternative actions being considered. But careful definition of the problem and consideration of objectives, followed by a calm, rational analysis of alternative courses of action, is calculated to produce a much better result than emotional, snap judgments which short-cut such economic reasoning.

This simple example illustrates in a crude way what we mean by an economic way of thinking—of making rational choices among alternatives. Of course, it is greatly oversimplified and makes no pretense of listing all of the alternatives or examining their consequences. Still, it helps to suggest how this general way of thinking about economic issues can be applied to most economic problems.

### The Role of Economic Analysis

In studying the functioning of the economic system and the relative merits of alternative economic policies, economics makes use of a set of analytical tools, just as do physics, engineering, the law, and other professions. In short, it depends upon a body of theory to provide a kit of tools with which to analyze the complexities of the real world. Some of these analytical tools and approaches are complex and difficult. But fortunately, some of the most valuable and powerful ones are simple and easily accessible without extensive formal training in economics. These are the ones that should be emphasized in the high schools.

An example is the so-called "Law of Supply and Demand." Economists have developed the concept of "demand," or "demand schedule," to refer to the different possible amounts of a product which people might buy at different possible prices during some specified period of time. (Thus, in general, more will be bought the lower the price.) There is also the parallel concept of "supply," which refers to the various amounts of a commodity that sellers would be willing to supply at different possible prices during some particular period of time. As a general rule, when more is demanded at some particular price than is being supplied at that price, the price will tend to be bid up by the excess demand until a new price is reached where the amount demanded just equals that being supplied.

Thus, economists have combined supply, demand, and price into a small "model" or "theory" of how the three will generally interact under prescribed conditions of competition. Such a model is useful for many practical problems. It tells us that if farmers grow more wheat this year than consumers are willing to buy at the present price, then the price of wheat will fall in the absence of government action. If the government wants to keep the price up, then it must be prepared to take the excess supply off the market.

Economics has many other comparable analytical tools designed to help us understand some part of the economic system. For example, a simple graphic device can be used to show how money income gives rise to spending and how such spending evokes a matching flow of goods and services. Consider this simple picture.

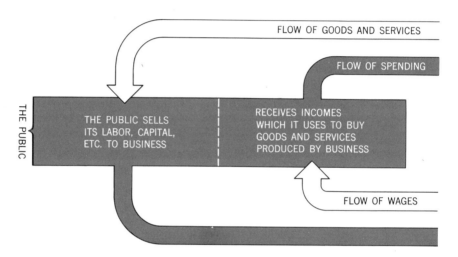

We see, on the right, that business firms hire productive services (workers, machines, raw materials, etc.), and that the payments they make for these services (wages, rents, interest, etc.) become the spendable incomes of the public. The public (on the left) in turn spends its income on the goods and services produced by business, creating the demands which business firms try to satisfy in their search for profits. Thus, there is a continuous flow of money payments from consumers to business and back to the public (consumers), matching a flow in the opposite direction of productive services and finished goods and services. Many real world complications are left out—most notably the government and saving—but the diagram presents a simple model of how money payments and goods and services flow through a private enterprise economy. The insights it provides can be helpful in the study of many economic problems such as inflation, which we used as an illustration in the preceding section.

166

These simple models of markets and of income flows can be expanded to include more elements of the real world. We can introduce the government, which diverts part of the income stream to itself through taxes and then replenishes the income stream through its spending. We can further complicate the model by introducing the banking system. The model is still an oversimplification of the modern American economy. It can, however, provide a useful framework for analyzing and evaluating the functioning of such an economy—a broad picture of the entire economic system.

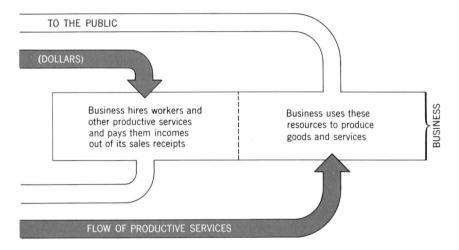

The important things to note about these models, or theories, are two. First, they try to isolate the main variables in a situation under study and to state some of the main relationships among these variables. Second, they simplify in order to highlight these main variables and relationships. Thus, they do not pretend to describe the real situation except in broad outline. They provide guides for thinking about particular situations or problems—not answers to them. They are tools of objective, rational analysis of how the economic system performs.

*The Importance of Careful Definitions and Terminology*

Much confusion in economic discussion arises because of failure to define the words being used. Careful definition of terms is essential to economic understanding and to rational discussion of economic issues. Little is gained by fighting over what is the best definition of a word. In principle, any definition can be used satisfactorily, so long as every-

167

one concerned understands what the terms mean. In practice, there is a major convenience in agreeing on commonly understood and widely used definitions.

Sometimes it is easy to agree on the definition of economic concepts. Thus terms like "gross national product" and "national income" have been given precise meanings by economists; these concepts as thus defined turn out to be very useful and are readily understood; and there is little disposition on anyone's part to argue about them (although some technical problems of measurement do arise). Other economic terms, however, are much less easy to define; and sometimes, even when we agree on a definition, it is not easy to fit our definition to the complexities of the real world.

"Capitalism," for example, is a term often used but seldom defined. Words so used are likely to generate more heat than light, especially when a complex situation is involved. And, even when we think we have agreed on a definition, difficulties of interpretation may remain.

Thus, most economists agree that a "capitalist" economy is marked by at least these major characteristics:

1. Private ownership of property prevails.
2. Large blocks of property have been accumulated by individuals and businesses, and this accumulated "capital" provides incomes to its owners.
3. Individuals and businesses are free to seek their own economic gain; the profit motive plays a central role in economic life.

The main requirement of such a definition is that it be clear and meaningful, but this alone is not enough to avoid difficulties of interpretation. For example, how free must individuals be to own and use property if a system is to be termed "capitalism"? How free must individuals be to seek their own economic gain? Does a federal law that limits the degree of monopoly power that a "capitalist" can acquire violate the tenets of capitalism? Is government operation of the postal system enough to make a society "noncapitalist"? Thus, many people may be prepared to accept the above definition of capitalism but yet disagree among themselves as to how "capitalist" the American economy actually is.

Economists do not have simple, universally accepted definitions for all important economic institutions. But they agree that rational consideration of any economic problem requires at least an understanding of the definitions being used. We cannot talk intelligently about the functioning of an economic system if the same term means different things or has drastically different connotations to different people.

Thus, a major step in rational, objective thinking about economic problems is clear definition and understanding of the important terms being used, although, as we have seen, agreement on definitions may not prevent disagreement in interpretation.

*Summary*

In this chapter we have emphasized the need for careful and logical thinking about economic questions. In Chapter III, we shall suggest the particular topics in economics that might be taught in high school —what big economic issues deserve emphasis, the functions every economic system must perform, the kinds of simple analytical tools that will help the student to think his way through economic issues, and the more important economic facts and institutions with which every citizen should probably be familiar. Not all schools will be able to cover all the material we suggest. But if the high school student graduates with a reasonable command of a substantial part of what is presented in Chapter III, and if he has been taught to deal with economic issues rationally, we believe that he will be well on his way to having the degree of economic literacy necessary for good citizenship.

# THREE

## *Understanding the Economy: Essential Analysis, Facts, and Institutions*

This chapter is concerned with what we consider to be the minimal understanding needed for effective citizenship in the modern American economy. In describing this minimum, we shall organize the material around three key economic questions: What shall be produced and how? How much in total can be produced, and how fast shall we grow? And who shall get the goods and services that are produced? All economic systems face these three big problems. The purpose here is to suggest the institutions, facts, and analysis that are essential for a reasonable understanding of the modern economic system, not to suggest how the material should be presented in high schools. There are many alternative patterns of presentation, on some of which we comment below. Much depends upon the nature of the course in which the material is presented.

We emphasize that our purpose is only to sketch the minimal economic understanding needed for responsible citizenship. It is not our purpose to present a textbook or complete statement of the facts, institutions, and analytical concepts needed. Thus, we make no pretense of developing fully the points we suggest. This is the job of a good textbook or of other teaching materials.

We do not expect that all students in all schools will have the opportunity (and some will not have the ability) to absorb all that is suggested here. Each school and teacher will have to decide what should be taught, in what courses, and in what ways. The total body of material presented here represents an ideal which the high schools should seek to achieve for the largest possible number of students.

### The Fact of Scarcity

*The basic fact which every economic system faces, some much more than others, is scarcity—the lack of enough productive resources to satisfy all the wants of its members. This basic fact of scarcity gives rise to the need for economizing—that is, for allocating the available productive resources so as best to satisfy the wants of the people. A clear recognition of this fact is fundamental to economic understanding and rational decision-making.*

Since there are more competing wants than can be satisfied, some procedure is required for ranking or compromising the competing desires for what our scarce resources can produce. We must decide what is most important and what is to be foregone.

*In this process, the concept of opportunity (or alternative) cost is a central one.* If resources are used to satisfy one want, they cannot be used to satisfy another. Thus, the alternative use that is not met is, in a real sense, the cost of satisfying the want for which the resource *is* used. For example, labor or machinery used to manufacture typewriters cannot be used at the same time to produce bicycles. Resources used to meet the private demand for consumer goods are not available to meet such public needs as, for example, more and better education. Similarly, materials and manpower used to produce new factories and machines in order to increase *future* output cannot be used to make more autos or other goods for *current* consumption.

The same concept applies at the household level. Almost no one has all the income he needs to satisfy all his wants. Thus a hundred dollars spent on a new suit may mean foregoing a new stove for the kitchen. And a dollar saved may mean giving up another movie or some other item in current consumption. Thus, for individuals and for the economy as a whole, the cost of using resources (or dollars) for any purpose is, fundamentally, the alternative uses (or opportunities) which must be foregone.

If an economy does not fully use all of its productive resources—that is, if there is unemployment of men or machines—it is imposing on itself a greater degree of scarcity than is necessary. The cost of these idle resources is the additional goods and services that could have been produced. (There is also the additional social cost in the personal frustration that results when men and women wanting to work cannot find useful jobs. There may also be a cost in putting men back to work, as when those with obsolete skills must be retrained and possibly moved to another town before they can find jobs.)

The opportunity costs associated with scarcity also exist when artificial plenty of one commodity is created through the misallocation of resources. Agricultural surpluses which consumers will not buy at government supported prices provide our best known example. Taxpayers who provide the funds to buy up these surpluses forego other goods they might have bought, and the economy as a whole does without things that might have been produced if the surplus labor and capital in farming had moved into other industries. While our economy is the most affluent the world has known, it is still true that satisfying one public or private need means that some other want goes unfilled.

*Economic Systems—The Big Economic Problems*

Given this fact of scarcity, all economic systems (capitalist, communist, or any other) face the same basic economic problems:

1. How shall the economy use (allocate) its productive resources to supply the wants of its people? In common sense terms, *what* shall be produced and *how?*

2. How fast shall the economy grow, and how shall it obtain reasonably stable growth, avoiding both depression and inflations? In other words, *how much* shall be produced in total, and how many resources shall be devoted to increasing future capacity rather than to producing goods for current consumption?

3. How shall the economy distribute money incomes, and through them the goods and services it produces, to the individual members and groups in society? For whom shall the goods be produced?

*Different economic systems solve these problems differently.* In our basically private-enterprise, market-oriented economy, consumers largely determine what shall be produced by spendng their money in the marketplace for those things they want most. Private businessmen produce the goods which consumers want to buy because in that way they make the largest profits, and competition with other businessmen exerts pressure on them to produce efficiently (at lowest cost). At the other extreme, in a completely planned and centrally directed economy, government officials determine what is to be produced, and administrative controls or force may be used to see that the goods are produced efficiently.

*In fact, most economies are mixed, neither purely private enterprise nor socialist (or communist), neither purely controlled by individual spending nor centrally directed.* Thus, in the American economy today, the great bulk of our productive activity is carried on by private, profit-motivated businesses, largely guided by the demands of millions of individual consumers. But federal, state, and local governments tax away and disburse about a quarter of the public's total income each year, and thus to that extent control what is produced and who gets it. Moreover, the people direct federal, state, and local governments to exercise a wide variety of controls over the economic activities of both businesses and individuals. In contrast, the major decisions in Russia on what shall be produced are made by the communist leaders. And most productive resources are owned by the state. But individuals earn incomes by working for pay, and they are generally free to buy what they wish with these incomes, subject to the over-all availability of goods set by the central planners.

In India and in China, still different mixes of private enterprise and central planning are used. One of the most important and difficult decisions that any society must make is what particular mixture of public and private activity it will use. It is important to recognize that while different economic systems set their goals and manage the allocation of their resources very differently, in many respects they differ only in degree as to how they solve their economic problems. To repeat, they all face the same central problem of scarcity—how to make the best use of scarce resources in satisfying competing needs.

*Most economic systems are not only "mixed" in the way they set their goals and manage their resources, they are also constantly changing.* The role of government in the American economy today is much larger than it was fifty years ago. Labor unions now play a major role in labor-management relations, whereas they were of small importance until the 1930's. Again, the structure of our banking system and the degree of government control over it have changed radically.

Likewise, the United Kingdom during the past half century has experienced a major swing from a basically private enterprise to a socialist economic philosophy. More recently there has been a partial swing back toward greater reliance on private enterprise—but still with more government participation in economic life than we have in America.

Russian communism has also undergone rapid and large changes in economic practice. Increasing reliance has been placed on money wages as the major incentive for individual workers and managers. Central planning of output has been relaxed somewhat and decentralized, and prices have come to play an increasingly important role. But major decisions on the division of output between consumers and capital goods, and such matters as the rate of economic growth remain firmly in the hands of the communist leaders. Clearly, one of the most difficult decisions any people must make is on the best balance between the public and private sectors of their economy.

Since different people want economic systems to achieve different goals, they understandably differ on how well their and other economies work. As between the communist leaders and most Americans, this point is obvious. But even within American society, economic goals differ widely. Some value individual freedom most highly. Others stress security, or rapid economic growth, or maximum output of goods and services. Some believe incomes should be distributed more equally, others less equally. In a democratic society, everyone has an equal right to his own views—and by the same token a special responsibility to have informed views rather than opinions based on ignorance and prejudice.

Thus, it is understandable that wide differences arise as to how the economic system should be modified to achieve better one or another of these goals. Economic analysis and understanding can aid straight thinking on such questions. But it cannot tell anyone what economic goals he should place highest—or that the goals held by someone else are "wrong."

## How the Economic System Uses Productive Resources in Satisfying Competing Wants

*An Overview of the Way the System Allocates Resources*

It is fair to say that most students do not understand, even in broad terms, how a basically private enterprise economy sets its priorities and uses its resources in achieving those goals—how it decides *what* to produce and *how* to produce it. If they do not understand this process, they cannot have very intelligent views about such important questions as how the consumer can get the most satisfaction out of his income, what conditions lead business firms to produce efficiently, the nature and causes of the "farm problem," the effects of economic concentration and monopoly, or the effects of raising or lowering tariffs, to cite only a few.

*In a basically private enterprise economy, consumers' money de-*

mands largely determine what is produced. Businessmen, striving to make profits, try to produce those goods and services which consumers want, and to do so at the lowest possible cost, sometimes also seeking to influence demand through advertising and other selling activities. The profit motive, operating under competitive pressures, largely determines how goods are produced—with what kinds of machinery, with how much labor, etc. In trying to maximize profits, businesses draw productive resources (such as labor, land, and machinery) into those occupations where they will contribute most to meeting consumer demands; and they pay out incomes to workers, landowners, and other suppliers of productive services. These incomes, in turn, make it possible for consumers to buy the goods they want. (This is the circular flow of incomes shown on pages 166 and 167) Markets, in which prices rise and fall in response to relative demands and supplies, provide the links which mesh together the entire set of consumers and businessmen, each seeking to make the best of his own position and abilities. Thus, it is the demands of individual consumers, coupled with the desire of businessmen to maximize profits (subject to broad social and legal controls) and the desire of individuals to maximize their incomes (consistent with their preferences as to working conditions, occupations, and so on), which together determine what shall be produced and how resources are used to produce it. (This section temporarily omits the government as a channel for establishing social priorities and for controlling the use of resources.)

It is important that students understand the central role which markets and prices play in this process. The market provides a mechanism by which consumers' demands can be expressed and responded to by producers. It is the need to pay a price that shuts some consumers out of the market at any time. If the commodity is in short supply relative to the demand, the price will be bid up and more consumers will be shut out. If, on the other hand, producing more of a commodity results in lowering its cost, this will tend to increase the amount supplied, whicn will lower the price and permit more consumers to buy the product. Thus price is everywhere the regulator in a private-enterprise, market-type economy.

*Some Important Facts and Concepts Concerning Resource Use*

In order to understand the functioning of a basically private enterprise economy along the above lines, it is desirable that students have a good grasp of at least the following central points:

*The stock of productive resources possessed by the American economy.* Resources are commonly classified into labor, capital (the stock of man-made productive resources, such as machines, buildings, and equipment), natural resources, and entrepreneurship (the function of managerial innovation and risk-taking). Students should have a general picture of the national stock of such resources, and of the way in which this stock has grown over the years. And they should have some impression of how our stock of resources compares to that of some of the other major nations. But while some factual knowledge about these matters is desirable, teachers must guard against the too common tendency merely to describe, classify, and memorize without understanding.

*The process of converting resources into goods and services which satisfy human wants.* Resources can satisfy human wants only by being combined and altered, which is what takes place in factories, mines, laboratories, and stores. It is important to recognize that economic production includes satisfying *all* wants for which consumers will pay, not merely production in the physical sense of converting resources from one tangible form to another. Thus, baking bread is clearly production, but so equally is transporting the bread from the bakery to the local store where the housewife can buy it. Similarly, the service of the banker, who uses labor and capital to provide checking and lending facilities, is production. So are the storage services of the grain elevator. The test of economic production is whether or not it uses resources to satisfy a human want for which someone will pay, not whether the action is morally good or bad.

*The factors involved when an economy converts its resources into desired goods and services.* Among the more important are the extent to which division of labor has been developed, the extent of technological progress, the quality and quantity of capital goods relative to the supply of labor and of natural resources, the quality of the labor supply (education, skills, and age level), the quality of entrepreneurs, and the general political and social environment (stability of government, observance of laws, and public attitudes). Students should see that the high American standard of living depends on a combination of all these factors, but here again the teacher should avoid putting too much emphasis on detailed factual description.

Some concepts deserve special attention. One of these is *"labor productivity."* Labor productivity is the foundation for high American wages and generally for the high American standard of living. This measure, which simply divides total output by the number of workers or by the total number of hours worked, does not imply that all this output is due to the efforts of labor, since it includes equally the efforts of management and the contributions of natural resources and man-made capital.

Moving to somewhat more difficult concepts, the student should understand the relationships between *saving, investment,* and *capital formation.* Saving may be in money or in "real" terms. In money terms, saving is the portion of individual or business income which is not spent on consumption. In "real" terms, saving (or investment) represents that portion of the economy's current output of new goods and services that is not used up in current consumption or in replacing wearing-out plants and machinery, but instead takes the form of new capital goods which represent a net addition to the economy's capacity to produce. This increase in buildings, machinery, and equipment, which enlarges the economy's productive capacity, is called "investment" or "capital formation." Capital formation through saving, because it does increase productive capacity, is a major means of increasing an economy's total output over time. Russia's rapid economic growth in recent years, for example, has been due largely to the very large fraction of its national income that has gone into capital formation rather than into consumption.

Students should be able to see how their own and their families' saving activities are related to the capital formation that takes place in the economy as a whole—how personal savings are channeled through the financial markets to business firms, homebuilders, and the like, who are thus given the means to employ resources which otherwise would have had to be used to produce more consumers' goods.

Students should also understand, in broad terms, the *principle of diminishing returns.* This principle states crudely, that when more of one productive resource (for example, labor) is combined with a fixed amount of another (for example, natural resources) under any given state of technology, the output per unit of the first will after some point diminish. An important real world application occurs in the plight of the underdeveloped countries with rapidly growing populations. If these countries have a substantially fixed or slowly increasing supply of natural resources and capital goods, then rapid growth of

177

population is not likely to be matched by a proportional increase in total output, with the result that output per capita declines. This represents the principle of diminishing returns at work. Students should see that this law can be offset by improvements in technology, as has been spectacularly true in the United States, where output per worker has risen steadily in spite of rapid growth in population over the last century.[1]

### The Role of Incentives, Competition, and Markets

*It is important for students to see that there are three main types of participants in economic activity. Each has an important role to play, and how effectively each performs its role depends largely on the nature of the economic incentives made available to it. These three groups of participants in the economic process are: Households (as consumers and as suppliers of productive services), business firms (which hire productive services and pay out incomes), and governments.*

The incentives to which these different groups react are different. Broadly speaking, the incentive of households is to sell their productive services (labor, land, capital) for the highest incomes they can obtain —subject to individual preferences about occupations, working conditions, and location—and to obtain the largest possible amount of desired goods and services by spending their incomes (with saving for the future as one possible use of income). Broadly speaking, businesses endeavor to earn as much profits as possible, operating within broad social and legal "rules of the game." In the case of governments, it is not particularly useful to speak of incentives. Governments are agents of the people and, at least roughly, reflect the people's wishes.

*Individual freedom of choice is central to the "private enterprise way."* It is essential that students understand both what this freedom does and does not mean, and also how a private enterprise economy manages to get its business done when individuals are free to make their own economic decisions. Students need to be reminded that, within fairly wide limits, the consumer is free to spend his money as

---

[1] Here, as in many cases, how precisely the economic principle is stated should depend upon the quality of the students and on the course in which the material is presented. Instructors can readily find more precise statements in college textbooks or in the better ones prepared for high school use. More precise analysis is desirable for superior students, but a rough statement can serve a useful general purpose for most students.

he wishes, the resource owner is free to employ his resources as he desires, and the businessman may seek profits where he pleases.

But the student should also understand that all these freedoms are limited, by laws and by social and moral pressures, for the protection of the individual and society. For example, households and businesses are not free to break legal contracts or to engage in fraud. They cannot freely allocate all of their income, since they must pay part of it to the government in taxes (for which they have voted). Businessmen may not collude to raise prices to customers, interfere with the rights of workers to organize their unions, or engage in a wide variety of practices specifically forbidden by law. Nor, as a practical matter, may they violate widespread social and ethical norms. The freedom of choice of business firms is subject to considerably wider controls than that of households. Freedom means different things to different people, and these basic value differences lead to disagreements on how well the present economic system does its job.

*Prices, reflecting shifting demand and supply conditions, are the main regulator of the allocation of scarce resources into production of the most desired goods and services.* It is this impersonal system of prices, operating on the incentives of households and business firms, which induces the participants in economic activity to act in such a way as to bring about this result. To understand how this process works, students will need a good command of the material in the following paragraphs.

In general, when consumers want more of anything, they will spend more of their income on it. This will bid up prices and increase potential profits in the production of the commodity. This in turn will induce businesses to produce more of it, perhaps luring new producers into the market. Such increased production will involve increased use of productive resources (labor, natural resources, capital, and enterpreneurship) in the production of this commodity, thereby bidding productive resources away from less desired commodities. As production (supply) is increased the price will generally come down again. This will make the commodity available to more consumers and at the same time lessen the incentive to expand further production. Substantially the opposite chain of consequences ensues from a fall in consumer demand for any product. Thus, broadly speaking, prices, reflecting the interaction of shifting demands and supplies in the market, serve as the regulator of economic activity in a basically private enterprise system.

179

*For a private enterprise economy to work well, competition in the market is essential.* Competition among sellers drives the price down toward the lowest figure consistent with covering total cost of production, including a reasonable profit for sellers. Without such competition, the profit incentive of businesses may lead to higher prices and higher profits with less goods for consumers, rather than more goods at the lowest price consistent with covering costs and reasonable profits. Thus, effective competition in markets is a necessary condition if a basically private enterprise system is to allocate resources effectively in accordance with consumer demands.[1]

*To comprehend the working of markets, the student must understand the main determinants of demand and supply.* (A wealth of everyday examples can be used to help him acquire this understanding.) Consumer demand for any product (the amounts that will be bought at different prices in any given market within a given period of time) reflects consumers' preferences. Given free choice, we can presume that people spend their dollars to obtain the things they want most. Consumers' demand for each product depends upon their preferences for it relative to competing products, the level of consumer income, and the price of the particular product relative to what alternative purchases might cost. Generally, consumers will buy more of any product the lower its price. But how much purchases will increase when price declines (i.e., how "elastic" demand is) varies widely from product to product and consumer to consumer. Business demands for productive services depend on different factors, primarily the contribution those services can make toward increasing output or reducing costs. But the concept of demand is a similar one for business firms and consumers.

A parallel concept of supply indicates the amounts that will be supplied in any given market during any particular time period at different possible prices. The supply of any product will, over the long run, depend largely on its cost of production relative to the price that can be obtained for it. This is because businesses will produce more of things that can be sold at a profit, but less of things that can not.

In discussing the functioning of a private enterprise system with

---

[1] By "competition" in this context we do not mean all kinds of economic rivalry, some forms of which (for example, excessive advertising and other selling costs) may result in increasing prices.

their students, teachers should be careful to make clear what it cannot do as well as what it does do well. Thus competitive markets, no matter how well they function, cannot satisfy consumers' wants unless these wants are backed by the ability to pay the price set in the market. Competitive markets are not an effective way of meeting broadly felt needs of great social usefulness that do not readily reflect themselves (for various reasons) in individual consumer demands. This is why we do not rely on private enterprise for police and fire protection, provision of national defense, elementary and secondary education, and other services provided by local, state, and federal governments.

## Modern Business, Economic Concentration, and Monopoly

We have seen that for a private enterprise economy to work well competition in markets is essential. Effective competition requires a substantial number of sellers and buyers in each market, plus reasonably effective information among buyers as to the nature of a product and its availability. For competition to serve its purpose in helping to allocate resources effectively, prices must be reasonably flexible, so they will move up and down in response to changes in consumer demand and changes in supply (cost) conditions. Competition may take the form of competition on quality as well as on prices, and quality competition has become increasingly important in the modern economic system. Introduction of new products and methods of production and the sifting out of the inefficient are also important parts of the competitive process.

Where effective competition is absent, economists apply the term monopoly or quasi-monopoly. At the extreme, there may be only one seller of a particular goods in a particular market (for example, the local water company). More commonly, however, there are at least a few sellers in a market, perhaps a small number of sellers producing closely related but not identical products (for example, the few large automobile companies or, at the local level, the dress shops in a particular shopping area). Businesses often strive through advertising and other selling activities to increase their share of markets and to differentiate their products from those of rivals, so as to be able to raise prices and make larger profits. Students should realize that advertising, and other related selling costs, may provide benefits to consumers, and also that these costs may increase the prices he pays.

181

*Where monopoly exists to an appreciable degree (in the markets for goods or for labor), society cannot rely on the market to bring about the most effective allocation of resources in response to consumer demands.* In general, where monopoly exists, production will be restricted and prices will be higher than under more competitive conditions.

Modern technology has complicated the problem of preserving effective competition, since in some instances businesses must be very large to attain the low costs which come with mass production. Thus, if market demand will only support one or a few firms big enough to take full advantage of modern technology, the presence of many business firms in the market will not necessarily produce the lowest possible price. But where only a few firms are in the market, history suggests there is a danger they will not compete effectively to push prices down to reflect the lowest possible cost. This poses a serious dilemma, and one which students can usefully debate among themselves.

*The problem of enforcing reasonable competition is thus a complex and difficult one.* Especially where modern technology requires that firms be large to obtain the advantages of low-cost mass production (for example, in the automobile, plate glass, and steel industries), it may be impossible to maintain large numbers of sellers in the market except at unduly high costs of production. The courts (and economists) generally try to evaluate each particular situation on its merits, in the light of the broad rules of legislation and the general goal of economic efficiency.

*The federal government plays a major role in enforcing competition through the anti-trust laws.* The Sherman Act, the Clayton Act, the Federal Trade Commission Act, and other federal laws are designed to prevent monopoly that will injure consumers and to insure the benefits of competition. Students should know something of the intent and nature of laws designed to enforce competition, and should understand something of the process by which such legislation is enforced through the courts and federal administrative agencies. But they need not know the history or content of the acts in detail.

*Over the past century there has been some tendency toward greater economic concentration, but the general structure of industry has remained relatively stable.* While all firms have grown larger on the average, there has been a substantial increase in the number of small firms as well as a growing number of very large ones. What is perhaps more important, improvements in transportation and communication have, for most products, turned the entire nation into one giant national market. The local market in which one or two small producers were protected from the competition of firms in other areas by high transportation costs has tended to disappear. Thus, although firms have grown larger, they compete over wider areas, and local monopolies are less common than they were a century or more ago. Students should be familiar with these trends in a general way and, particularly in their history courses, should have the opportunity to look briefly at the development of trusts, holding companies, and other forms of mergers over the past century.

Business firms seek to become large for a variety of reasons. Large-scale production usually brings lower costs, and the bigger the company the more likely it is to have some degree of (monopoly) power in its market. This does not mean that large firms are always successful. Sometimes bigness brings inefficiency. How large a firm needs to be to attain maximum efficiency varies widely from industry to industry. Even when a company has a plant of just the right size, it may continue to expand by building or acquiring additional plants—in order to increase its power in the market, to diversify its production by adding new products, to increase its financial strength, or for other reasons.

*Many people are concerned about the economic and political consequences of bigness in business, quite aside from the considerations of economic efficiency resulting from lack of effective competition.* Big businesses have extensive economic power over those who work for them and over their customers, though this power is limited by competition with other big businesses for both customers and productive resources, and by the power of workers organized into large labor unions. Some observers believe that big businesses exert improper political power. In recent years, similar fears have been expressed regarding the economic and political power of labor unions. Other organized groups may also wield considerable political power in matters affecting their economic interests.

*Where monopoly is obviously inescapable, the public has generally authorized regulated "public utilities."* A public utility is an organization producing a product considered to be a necessity, under conditions where competition would clearly be to the public disadvantage, and where the government therefore gives a legal monopoly subject to government control over prices charged and services rendered. Examples are local water, electricity, and gas companies. In such cases, the economies of large-scale production provide service at lower cost to the public. But in return for giving the monopoly privilege, the public reserves the right to regulate the price the company may charge and to prescribe the kinds of service it must render. The use of regulated public utilities is an alternative approach to the problem of monopoly. It has been widely accepted where competition cannot be counted upon to bring an adequate supply of desired goods to consumers at a reasonable price.

*In the modern American economy, the corporation is the dominant form of business organization.* Students should know something about the organization of the corporation and about its financing through stocks and bonds as means of mobilizing capital from the general public. (They need not, however, be exposed in detail to the many forms of corporate securities or the elaborate forms of corporate financing.) In large corporations, with widely held stock, stockholders often exert little control over the operating policies of the corporation. Thus managements tend to be self-perpetuating and under little direct control from the rank and file of stockholders. Not only is there a concentration of power and wealth in large firms, but also power within these firms is concentrated in the hands of a relatively small number of executives and large stockholders. Where this occurs, important problems of social policy are raised.

In connection with corporations, it is desirable for students to have a grasp of a *simple* balance sheet and income statement, reflecting only the four or five major categories in each. This should provide some foundation for understanding the relationship between assets, liabilities, and proprietorship in the corporation balance sheet, and between sales income and major elements of cost in the profit and loss statement. It is probably undesirable for students to be exposed to the complexities of major corporate financial statements at this stage unless considerable time is allocated to their study.

Students should also understand the important function performed by securities exchanges, which permit investors to buy and sell readily securities which have already been issued. Because the stock exchange provides a smoothly functioning market, many people are willing to invest some of their savings in securities, which they can later sell readily if the need should arise. Because this market exists, business firms find it easier to raise capital from (sell securities to) a broad public. However, there is no need for the student to devote much time to studying the detailed workings of the stock exchange and the time some students are required to spend pretending to buy and sell stocks could often be better used in the kinds of economic analysis suggested in these pages.

## Government and the Allocation of Resources
## (Taxes and Government Spending)

*It is important, for students to understand that, even in a basically free enterprise economy, governments play a significant role in setting priorities and using resources—that is, in deciding what to produce and how to produce it.* The economic functions of governments fall into three broad groups—regulatory; reallocation of resources and incomes through taxes and expenditures; and activities designed to affect the rate of economic growth and to avoid economic instability. The regulatory function makes little direct use of productive resources, though it may have a far-reaching impact on the private use of resources in the economy. Regulation occurs in many ways beyond those indicated above in preventing monopoly. For example, government intervenes to encourage or require farmers to limit output so as to raise farm prices and incomes; it supports "fair trade" practices which reduce the freedom of retailers to cut prices on "fair-traded" products; it establishes zoning regulations that limit the uses to which land can be put; it sets maximum working hours and minimum safety regulations. Examples could be multiplied.

We concentrate, however, in this section on government actions which directly reallocate resources. Direct government participation in the allocation of productive resources and incomes occurs largely through public expenditures which bid resources away from private use, and through the imposition of taxes to obtain funds for those expenditures.

*In a fully employed economy, use of resources in the public sector necessarily implies a diversion of resources from the private sector.* Thus government use of resources is an alternative to private use. Decisions on taxes and government spending are one major way in which we decide how to manage our economic resources, instead of relying on the private sector of the economy. Public expenditures are justified if they contribute more to the public welfare than do private expenditures of the same amount. In the United States we decide largely through the political process what resources to use in the public sector and how to use them, in contrast to major reliance on private spending in the private sector.

*Government expenditures and taxes have grown rapidly over the past century.* Students should have some impression of the order of magnitude of government spending, which now accounts for over a quarter of the national income. Somewhat over half of this is federal spending, while the rest is divided between state and local expenditures. Students should also have a broad picture of the major types of expenditures—for example, the fact that defense and defense-related expenditures account for about two-thirds of total federal outlay, and for around half of the total spending of all governments—federal, state, and local. They should also recognize the force of population growth and increased demand for public services in causing persistent increases in government expenditures.

*In the American economy, government services have been largely limited to activities which people believe cannot be effectively provided through the private sector of our type of economy.* Major examples are the provision of national defense and general government services, such as police and fire protection. Governments also provide many other services (like education and highways) which might be provided through the marketplace on a profit basis, but which could not in this way be made generally available at reasonably low prices for the general public. Most government services are of sorts on which it is difficult to place a market value for the individual user—for example, national defense and education. They are provided on a non-price basis, though this is not always true. Such services as water, electricity, and use of toll roads are provided only in response to direct payment by the user. In cases like these user payments may just cover costs, or they may involve a government deficit or surplus in operating the activity. Governments also participate in intermediate ways in providing services—for example, by providing funds at low interest rates to stimulate rural electrification.

*There is considerable disagreement as to whether the public sector should be larger or smaller than it now is.* Americans generally dislike to give up personal control over the spending of their incomes, as they must do when they pay taxes. But many feel that as the nation grows wealthier, we ought to devote a larger proportion of our resources to education, conservation, national defense, and other such activities that can effectively be provided for general use only through government activities.

*Taxes are the main means of diverting incomes (and hence control over resources) from the private to the public sector of the economy.* Taxes take spending power away from individuals and businesses and give this spending power to governments. When a family pays its income or property taxes, its potential spending on such things as food, autos, or clothing is reduced. When the government spends the tax money on roads or missiles, productive resources are drawn away from the things consumers buy to produce roads, missiles, and other things for public use. In most cases, governments directly divert resources from the private to the public sector of the economy. In some instances, however, governments make expenditures which merely transfer the dollars to individuals or businesses without requiring that productive services be rendered in return. Examples of such government "transfer payments" are unemployment and old-age benefit payments, and various types of public assistance.

Students should have a general impression of the major taxes currently used. These include the personal income tax, the corporation income tax, sales taxes, payroll taxes, and property taxes. This knowledge should include an impression of the relative importance of the different taxes and a little about their operation—but not detailed analysis of each.

Some major characteristics of taxes which deserve attention are their progressiveness (the extent to which they fall on higher or lower income groups), their incidence (who ultimately bears the burden), and their effects on incentives to work and invest. Students should recognize the importance of these features in evaluating different taxes.

### The International Allocation of Resources—International Trade

*The United States is increasingly tied to the rest of the world, in economic as well as political matters. Hence it is important that the student be introduced to the study of international economic relations.* We recognize that this involves dealing with some material which high school students will find difficult. Teachers will need to select carefully the material that they hope to cover.

*The basic case for specialization and exchange among nations is the same as the case for them within a nation—that with specialization and exchange a larger total quantity of wanted goods and services can be produced with a given supply of productive resources.* Climatic and geographical conditions vary widely over the face of the earth. So do human capacities. Moreover, the accumulated supply of capital goods varies greatly from nation to nation, and the proportions among different types of resources vary widely. Lastly, great differences exist in the political and social climate in different countries. All these considerations strengthen the argument that the total output of goods and services in the world will be larger if different countries specialize in the production of particular goods and services and if there is free exchange among nations. When total world output is increased by specialization and free international trade, all nations gain but the gain to some countries may be greater than to others.

*An important difference between international and domestic trade arises from the fact that different nations use different currencies.* This complicates the problem of making international payments, since citizens of each country generally want payment in their own currency. An elaborate financial mechanism has grown up to convert currencies of different nations into one another. The rate at which one currency can be bought with another is called the "rate of exchange." For example, if one British pound will buy $2.80 in the foreign exchange market, the exchange rate is said to be 2.80 to 1.

*Students should be given a brief introduction to the concept of the international balance of payments. This is a summary statement of all the payments one country makes to others and of the payments it receives from other countries during some period of time, say, a year.* Thus, when Americans export goods abroad, provide shipping or insurance services for foreigners, or receive dividends and interest on their investments in other countries, then payments must be made to the United States. That is, foreigners have to use their own currencies to buy dollars to pay Americans. Conversely, Americans must use their dollars to buy foreign currencies in order to pay for imports of goods and services from other countries.

United States exports of goods and services ordinarily exceed our imports. Hence, other countries generally need to pay us more than we need to pay them. However, there are two other types of international transactions that have in recent years more than offset this net balance. First, American business firms and investors send large sums abroad to invest in other countries. These investments represent payments to other countries just as much as payments for imports. (Later on, payments will be made back to the United States in the form of interest and dividends.) Second, the American government has provided large amounts of military and economic aid to foreign nations.

188

This again requires that payments be made to other countries.

When we add everything up, including international investments and government aid, we find that in recent years the United States has had a *deficit* if its balance of payments; we have undertaken to pay more to other countries than they have had to pay to us. For a long time before this, we had a *surplus* in our balance of payments; other countries had to pay us more than we needed to pay them.

Teachers will do well if they can get this much across to their students. They should be careful to avoid becoming lost in the details of the balance of payments. If there is time, especially with the better students, they may wish to go further and consider how international deficits and surpluses are settled, which will give students a chance to study the role which gold plays as an international means of payment. Thus, if a country has a deficit in its balance of payments, one way of taking care of the problem is for it to pay the deficit in gold, which other countries are always prepared to accept. Payments deficits may also be settled in another way—by foreigners simply accepting deposits in American banks. This settlement does not involve current gold transfers, though foreigners may later decide to withdraw their deposits and use the dollars to purchase gold for export.

One point that should be emphasized with students is the difference between the *balance of trade* and the *balance of payments.* The former refers only to exports and imports of goods and services; the latter refers to *all* international payments, including those arising from international loans, government aid, and so on. The United States exports more than it imports. It has a surplus in its balance of trade. But, as we have just explained, it has in recent years had a deficit in its total balance of payments.

*Nations use tariffs and other restrictive devices to limit imports and to increase the excess of exports over imports.* Historically, there have been many reasons for adopting tariffs. Among the more important are the desire to protect new industries that are just getting started, the desire to become more self-sufficient in case of war, and, most important, the desire to provide more jobs for domestic workers and to protect domestic wages against the competition of workers in other nations receiving lower wages. American tariff history reflects all these desires, and until the 1930's our country was one of the leaders in raising tariffs. More recently, we have played an important role in trying to reduce tariff levels throughout the world.

189

*Although tariffs may give temporary advantages to the countries establishing them, they have generally led to retaliatory tariff increases by other nations and have reduced the total level of international trade. Most economists thus agree that the major result has been to lower rather than to raise total output and living standards in countries using tariffs.* Tariffs may protect employment in particular domestic industries. But they also reduce imports and thus cut off the ability of foreigners to buy our products in the export market. Thus, they allocate resources into relatively inefficient industries and away from those which would prosper most under free specialization, division of labor, and exchange. Hence, while tariffs may benefit particular groups, they generally do so at the expense of the national standard of living. Tariffs thus provide an excellent opportunity for students to apply the central principles of free market economics in a controversial area which points up the possible conflict between private group and general consumer interests—to see economic analysis as a tool kit of analytical concepts and a way of thinking about economic issues, rather than as a set of ready-made "answers" to economic problems.

---

## *Major Concepts and Institutions Introduced in This Section*

*Scarcity—the need for economizing*

*Costs—opportunity (or alternative) costs, money costs*

*Productive resources—factors of production*

*Division of labor, specialization, and exchange*

*Economic production—conversion of resources into desired output*

*Saving, investment, capital formation*

*Labor productivity*

*Principle of diminishing returns*

*Demand, supply, price*

*Market*

*Competition*

*Profit, profit incentive*

*Interdependence—the price and market system*

*Economic efficiency*

*Monopoly, anti-trust laws*

*Public utility*

*Corporation, balance sheet, profit and loss statement*

*Government expenditures and taxes in allocating resources*

*Taxes—corporate income tax, personal income tax, property tax, sales tax, payroll tax*

*International specialization*

*Balance of payments, balance of trade*

*Tariffs*

---

# Economic Growth and Stability

*The Importance of Economic Growth and Stability*

*Students need to be introduced to the fact that many of our greatest economic problems center around how to obtain stable economic growth, avoiding the excesses of the inflationary booms and depressions.* Depression and mass unemployment bring human misery and vast waste of potential output. Inflation erodes the value of savings and may lead to disruptive speculation and misallocation of resources. Every American voter will need to make up his mind on a host of major public policy issues arising from these problems—when to raise and lower taxes, and which taxes; what to do about the national debt; whether money should be "easy" or "tight"; whether the government should spend more or less to promote stability; whether to oppose or favor unemployment insurance; and many more. Added to all these in recent years has been increasing concern with the rate at which our economy grows. Many observers are concerned that our growth rate since World War II has been slower than that of Russia and many other leading industrialized nations.

*Economic stability and growth of total output are among our most important objectives.* They are broad goals on which virtually everyone agrees, although arguments do arise as to *how much* stability and growth we want and what we are prepared to pay in the possible sacrifice of other desired objectives. A prosperous economy, which provides jobs at good wages for all who want to work, is an economy with a high and steadily rising level of output. When production declines, so do incomes and jobs. All private-enterprise economies have in the past been afflicted with some degree of economic instability. Depressions have alternated with boom periods, and jobs have often not been available for all who wanted work.

*We want growth as well as stability.* Put as simply as possible, economic welfare depends on the level of output *per capita*. Economic progress depends on having national output grow faster than population increases. Increasing total output alone does not assure a rising average standard of living, unless population grows less rapidly.

*Measures of National Income and Production*

*The most widely used measure of total output today is known as the "gross national product,"* which measures the total production of goods and services during a given period. Students should be familiar with the concept, although technical details should be avoided. The gross national product (usually abbreviated GNP) is regularly computed and published by our government and that of most other advanced countries; it is reported in the daily press; and changes in the GNP are carefully followed by all those concerned with the functioning of the economy. Another important measure of over-all economic activity is the "national income." Part of the total GNP is needed to replace that part of an economy's stock of capital equipment which wears out (depreciates). The remainder of the GNP (after certain other adjustments) comprises the "national income," available for consumption or investment in expanding the nation's stock of capital. Every informed citizen should be reasonably familiar with these two measures of the nation's total output and income.

As we know all too well, prices of goods and services do not remain constant. The "price level" (which is an expression for how high or low prices are on the average) may rise or fall. Since the 1930's, it has risen very substantially, so that it now takes considerably more dollars to buy the same amount of goods. Thus, the *dollar value* of the nation's output may show a rise, if prices have increased, even though there has been no increase in the output of goods and services. It is important to distinguish between changes that reflect only changes in prices and those that represent a rise or fall in "real" output. For example, suppose that the GNP rises from 500 to 525 billion dollars, or by five per cent, at the same time that prices on the average rise by two per cent. Then the increase in the production of goods and services—in "real" GNP—is only three per cent. The remainder of the five per cent rise in the money value of GNP represents merely higher prices.

*Main Forces Determining National Production and Income*

*The upper limit to an economy's real output at any time is set by its stock of productive resources (labor, capital goods, and natural resources) and the technology it has for using these productive resources.* An economy may produce less than its total capacity permits; it can produce more only by increasing this capacity.

*The level of total output depends on the amount of total spending (effective demand) as well as on the economy's productive capacity.* In a profit-motivated economy, effective demand is not always large enough to call forth production at a full-capacity level. Businessmen in general only produce if they can sell their output at a profitable price. Thus, money demand must be large enough to buy all the goods the economy can produce if it is to operate at full capacity. Below the upper limit set by the economy's total productive capacity, output and employment may rise or fall as total spending on current output rises or falls. Hence it is essential that we understand something about the factors that determine the level of total spending.

*The total output of the economy is bought by three large groups of spenders: consumers, business firms, and governments.* (For simplicity, we neglect at this point the excess of our exports over our imports, which represents the net purchases of foreigners.) To understand why the level of output changes, we must know something about the forces that determine each of these types of spending.

*The largest part of the GNP is bought by consumers, whose spending is closely tied to their incomes.* But the relation between income and consumers' spending is not a rigid one, and variations in this relation have a significant effect on the level of economic activity.

*The most volatile component of private spending is that by businesses—for plant, equipment, and changes in their inventories of materials and finished goods. Private spending on housing (by both business and individuals) also fluctuates sharply.* The mild recessions in the United States since World War II have been largely associated with wide changes in business accumulation and decumulation of inventories. For example, in 1950-51, 1955-56, and 1959-60 businesses produced more than they sold, providing jobs and incomes but accumulating inventories rapidly. In 1953-54, 1957-58, and 1960-61 they produced less than they sold, drawing down their previously accumulated inventories as they cut back on production and employment. These declines contrasted with the more severe depressions of the past which were associated with large drops in business expenditures on plant and equipment and in residential building. This was particularly true in the great depression of the 1930's. Mild recessions have occurred frequently in the United States—usually every three or four years. But there have also been a few very long and severe depressions, especially in the 1870's, 1890's and 1930's, and some that have been severe but short-lived.

*Booms and depressions tend to feed on themselves because of the interdependence among different kinds of economic activity.* A decline in business investment leads to a fall in income, which causes

193

consumers' expenditures to decline. A rise or fall in the sales of one industry leads to repercussions on the production and sales of other industries, to corresponding changes in income and employment in these industries, and to still further changes in consumers' expenditure and business spending. Students need to be impressed with the fact that this element of *dynamic interdependence* is a highly important feature of all money-using, private-enterprise economies. Such interdependence also tends to tie together the economies of different nations that trade with each other.

### The Role of Government Budgets
### (Expenditures, Taxes, and Borrowing)

*We now realize much better than we did a few decades ago that government budget policy can play an important stabilizing role in a potentially unstable economy.* Government purchases of goods and services support the level of output and employment, just as does private spending. A rise or fall in private purchases can be offset by an opposite change in government spending. But government tax receipts also affect private spending; tax collections represent a reduction in the purchasing power of private spenders.

*The difference between the government's tax receipts and its spending represents the government's budgetary surplus or deficit.* A budgetary surplus means that tax receipts are larger than government expenditures; this ordinarily has a depressing effect on total spending. A government deficit means that government expenditures are larger than tax receipts; this ordinarily tends to expand total spending. Thus, the size of the budgetary deficit or surplus affects total spending and the level of total economic activity. This explains why economists are generally agreed that a government deficit may be helpful when private spending declines and a depression threatens, and similarly that a rising budgetary surplus can help to hold back a too rapid expansion in private spending. It is important that we understand, by careful economic reasoning, when it is desirable to have a balanced budget, and when not. While economists generally agree that government budget policy can help to lessen economic instability, there is considerable uncertainty as to how far such action can go toward avoiding serious instability.

*When the government spends more than it collects in taxes (creating a deficit), an increase in the public debt results.* Thus, government

194

One final point regarding both monetary and fiscal policy which is of considerable current importance, needs to be made here. *Both monetary and fiscal (budgetary) policy face difficult problems in trying to eliminate recession and unemployment on the one hand, and inflation on the other.* A serious dilemma arises particularly if inflation occurs at a time when substantial unemployment is present. Usually inflation reflects excess spending beyond the supply of goods available for current purchase; when this is the case, a budget surplus and tight money are generally appropriate anti-inflationary measures. But sometimes costs and selling prices are pushed up by strong labor unions and business firms when unemployment still exists. If this is the case, restrictive monetary and budgetary policy to check inflation may prevent further reduction of unemployment or even cause additional unemployment. This is a case in which costs and prices are being pushed up because of the power of strong economic groups, not because "too many dollars are chasing too few goods." Monetary and fiscal policy are thus much less effective in this kind of situation than when the inflation is clearly due to too much spending.

## The Problem of Economic Growth

*Economic growth is usually measured by the increase in output per capita.* In the United States, total real output has grown over the past century at about three per cent per annum or a bit more, although per capita output has grown only about two per cent per annum, since population has grown at a rate of about one per cent. This growth rate has been impressive compared to other nations over the long pull, but in recent years some other nations have grown at faster rates.

*The upper limit to economic growth is set by the growth in the capacity of the economy to produce.* Expansion in productive capacity depends mainly on growth in the labor force, improvement in the quality of labor, growth in the stock of capital, improvement in the quality of capital, and technological and managerial advance. A nation can increase its growth rate by increasing its productive capacity through any or all of these factors.

*Increase in productive capacity generally requires investment (increase in the stock of human and nonhuman capital).* As we have seen, this implies a diversion of resources from current consumption through saving into investment in order to build up the stock of capital. We must then use some of our steel to build new factories and highways to increase future output rather than autos and refrigerators for current consumption. We must also use some of our skilled manpower to teach others and to do research, rather than to make goods for current consumption. Generally those countries which have saved and invested the largest proportion of current output in capital accumulation have grown most rapidly. But education and technological advance (in both the engineering and managerial senses) appear to have been at least equally important in speeding economic growth in the western nations.

*Economic growth also depends on growth in effective demand (spending).* Actual output will grow in a basically private enterprise economy only as fast as effective demand for goods and services grows. Effective demand (total money spending) may exceed or fall short of the productive capacity of the economy at any time. Thus, a satisfactory growth of output requires a satisfactory growth in spending—by consumers, business, and government. This expansion in spending, over the long run, requires that the money supply must grow at something like the same rate, and this means that the banking system must be enabled to expand its deposits. For example, if our productive capacity grows at three per cent per annum, then, unless average prices decrease, total spending must also increase three per cent per annum if businessmen are to sell all the goods they can produce. And roughly, the money supply needs to increase something like three per cent to support the three per cent increase in total spending.

To obtain such a satisfactory growth in the money supply requires that either the private or the public sector of the economy must be increasingly in debt to the banking system to provide the needed increase in money under our present institutional arrangements. This is because the banks create money (deposits) by lending to business, individuals, and governments, who thereby go in debt to the banks. Thus, increases in debt are not necessarily bad in relation to the economy's need for an increasing money supply.

*But it is important to recognize that mere increases in money purchasing power do not necessarily speed economic growth if they exceed the rate of growth in real productive capacity. In that case, they may merely lead to inflation.*

## Growth and the Underdeveloped Economies

United States per capita output is far higher than in any other nation. About two-thirds of the world's population has a very low per capita output—generally estimated at less than $150 per year. In these so-called underdeveloped areas (of which India and China comprise over one billion people) poverty prevails. With very low income levels, substantial saving is difficult because all income is needed for current consumption. The underdeveloped economies therefore find it very hard to increase their stock of capital, either through education and improved skills for human beings, or through accumulation of non-human capital. Such economies generally have also an insufficient supply of enterprising managers and investors to make use of the best technological knowledge; and often political, social, and economic conditions prevail which discourage thrift and risk-taking. In most such nations total output is growing, but often no faster than the growth in population. Since the rate of population growth is often very high, "the population problem" keeps per capita output from rising. It is important for students to understand the vast difference between conditions here and in the underdeveloped economies, and to appreciate some of the problems such economies face.

*The present generation has seen a revolution in aspirations in the underdeveloped countries.* The people of the underdeveloped countries are becoming increasingly dissatisfied with their "backward" status. They are insisting on higher standards of living and on the means to achieve these higher standards. In these economies, many observers view private enterprise and communism as alternative paths toward higher standards of living. Every citizen needs to realize that these conditions prevail in much of the world and that there is no necessary predisposition toward the private enterprise solution in most of the underdeveloped areas in Asia, Latin America, Africa, and the poorer countries of Europe. An important feature of American foreign economic policy is the desire to aid the underdeveloped countries to achieve more rapid growth—through government loans and grants, encouragement of private investment in these areas, provisions of technical assistance, and so on.

---

## Essential Concepts and Institutions Introduced in This Section

Gross national product, national income, per capita product and income
Money and real income
Price level

Equation of exchange

Aggregate demand (total spending), and components of aggregate demand (consumer spending, business spending on investment, goverment spending)

Business cycle, depression, inflation

Money—bank deposits and money creation through bank lending

Central bank—Federal Reserve System

Government budget, fiscal policy, public debt

Economic growth

Underdeveloped areas

The population problem

Note that this section also re-uses many of the essential concepts introduced in the earlier section, such as saving and capital formation.

---

## The Distribution of Income

*The third big economic question which all economic systems must answer is: who shall receive the goods and services the economy produces, and in what proportions?* This is the question of "for whom" raised on page 170.

The distribution of income raises some of our most difficult economic issues. Are incomes distributed too unequally—should taxes fall more heavily on the upper income groups? Should wages get a bigger share of the national income relative to profits? Should we expand social security measures to provide incomes for retired persons and others not working and, if so, who should pay the bill? Should unions be encouraged or restricted in their attempts to raise wages?

*The money incomes people receive mainly determine the shares of the national output they obtain. In a private enterprise economy, most people receive money incomes as payments for the use of productive services they provide to business firms or the government.* Thus, workers receive wages for their labor; others receive rent, interest, or profits in return for providing natual resources, capital, or business ability. This process is illustrated by the circular flow diagram on pages 166 and 167 to which we have referred on several occasions.

Students should understand how money incomes arise out of the sale of productive services by individuals to businesses and governments. Equally important, they should understand that these money incomes provide the means of obtaining "real income"—that is, the goods and services that people buy with their money incomes. A household's income thus generally depends on the amount of productive services it can sell and on the price of these services.

*The four major classes of incomes are wages (and salaries), interest, rent, and profits.* Wages and salaries are payments for human productive services. Interest and rent are payments for the services of capital goods and natural resources. Profits generally represent a combination of payments for managerial services, entrepreneurial risk-taking, and the use of capital. In modern business, the exact definition of profits is complicated, but business profits in essence represent the difference between costs and total receipts from sales.

*In a private enterprise economy, people receive incomes roughly in proportion to the value which the market puts on the contributions they make to economic production.* Productive services which are in heavy demand to help produce goods and services wanted by consumers tend to be bid up in price; those for which the demand is small compared to supply tend to have a low price. It is important to remember that many people receive incomes from the productive services of accumulated (and also inherited) wealth which they own, not from human services which they themselves provide. Many of the largest incomes in the United States are based primarily on income from accumulated wealth in the form of dividends, interest, and rents.

Roughly two-thirds of the national income is paid in the form of wages and salaries, and one-third takes the form of profits, rents, and interest. The income of many households comes from both sources, but most households receive most of their income in the form of wages and salaries.[1]

*Personal Distribution of Income in the U.S.*

Average individual and family incomes in the United States are by far the largest of any nation in the world. A major economic development in the United States during the present century has been the growth of a large "middle class" of families which are not rich but which are reasonably well off. But the American economy still includes a large number of extremely poor families and some very rich

---

[1] Much of the "profit" received by owners of small unincorporated firms (including farms) is really a return on the owners' labor, even though the income is reported as profits.

families. Students should know in broad outline of the distribution of personal incomes in the United States, including their own place in the income structure.

While the personal distribution of income has been relatively stable during the present century, there has been a gradual tendency for a smaller proportion of total personal income to go to the highest income groups. For example, the fraction of total income going to the top ten per cent of families both before and after taxes has dropped appreciably since 1929. This gradual reduction of inequality in the United States has a number of causes: highly progressive income taxes, heavy inheritance taxes, the growing strength of labor unions, government efforts to help the lowest income groups, and some decline in the relative importance of rent and interest. Thus, in the United States (and in most other wealthier countries) incomes have tended to become somewhat more equally distributed.

Nonetheless, poverty continues to exist on a substantial scale in the United States. For example, in 1960 apparently about fifteen per cent of all families (excluding unattached single persons) received money incomes of less than $2,000. This poverty reflects partly the presence of many individuals who have no valuable productive service which they can sell—for example, retired persons, widowed or divorced mothers with small children, uneducated persons with low skills, persons disabled or in ill health, and other such groups. Partly, it reflects the presence of substantial groups who are temporarily or permanently unemployed, including those unable or unwilling to move out of areas of unemployment left by declining industries. Partly it reflects the lack of adequate job opportunities for Negroes and other minority groups. Poverty tends to be concentrated in particular geographical areas and within particular groups of the population.

*Significant inequality in personal incomes exists in all societies.* This income inequality tends to be substantial in private enterprise economies in part because such economies encourage the accumulation of capital, and such capital accumulations produce large incomes for their owners. Differences in ability and opportunity also contribute to the spread between low and high incomes. Unequal distribution of income also prevails in the underdeveloped countries to an extreme extent, with a few very rich and great masses of very poor. In the communist countries inequality is less than in the private enterprise economies, because there is little personal income from accumulated capital.

But incomes received from wages and salaries may be as unequal, or even more unequal, than in the private enterprise economies.

## Labor, Wages, and Labor Unions

*Students should understand that high American wages rest fundamentally on the high productivity of American labor.* Although many factors influence individual wages at different times, producers can only pay wages justified by the productivity of workers if they are to continue in operation and make reasonable profits over the long run. If businesses cannot make reasonable profits, they will cease to exist in private enterprise economies. Competition among businesses for workers will tend to bid wages up to roughly the level justified by the productivity of the workers. While these tendencies are broad and inexact, it is clear that productivity as valued in the market is the major force establishing the level of wages for workers with different abilities in the American economy.

*It is real wages, not money wages, that determine how well off workers are.* Students should understand this distinction clearly. If money wages rise no faster than prices, real wages do not rise at all. Very roughly, *real* wages in the United States are close to five times as high as they were sixty years ago. This is the result of the rapid increase in labor productivity that has occurred. *For real wages to continue to rise, it is necessary that labor productivity also continue to increase.*

*Labor productivity may rise both from the activities of workers themselves and from the accumulation of capital and technological and managerial advance.* The high productivity of American workers depends on their superior education, their accumulated skills, and their work habits. It also results from the fact that they have the largest accumulation of capital goods (plants, machinery, and equipment) in the world with which to work, and on the advanced state of American technology and management. Thus workers, managers, and investors can reasonably expect to share in the nation's growing output.

*Over the past century, and especially since the 1930's, workers have increasingly organized themselves into labor unions to improve their bargaining power vis-a-vis employers.* Without unions, individual workers would often be in a weak bargaining position against large employers. Since the 1930's federal law has supported the right of workers to organize into unions of their choosing, with which employers must bargain collectively over wages, working conditions, and other such questions of common interest to workers and their employers. Unions have pressed for higher wages, shorter working hours, and better working conditions, and more recently for improved pension plans and other such "fringe benefits." There is no doubt that unions have improved the strength and the general position of workers in the American economy. But there is considerable disagreement as to the extent to which they have actually raised real wages. Unions and employers generally agree that unions have raised wages at the expense of profits, compared to a nonunion economy, but objective studies by economists leave this issue in doubt.

Every person should understand something of the role of unions in labor-management relations. Unions represent workers on a wide variety of issues. Strikes supported by union picketing represent the most powerful union weapon, but strikes occur infrequently. Most differences are settled peaceably through collective bargaining. Public support for labor unions has varied considerably as the apparent strength of unions compared to management has changed, and laws in relation to unions are under constant discussion. Such issues as the "closed shop" and "right-to-work laws" are worth brief student attention.

Problems like "featherbedding," monopolistic output restrictions by management, and restrictive tariffs provide excellent opportunities for students to apply the central proposition that high wages and other incomes depend basically on high real output. They also provide an excellent opportunity to understand how conflicts arise between private group interests on the one hand and the general welfare on the other. Students should understand that economic groups obtain their income objectives partly through the political process as well as through the marketplace. The fact that these issues are controversial is all the more reason why they should be objectively discussed in the classroom.

*Farm Incomes—the "Farm Problem"*

On the average, farm incomes are considerably below those of the nonfarm portion of the economy. Within the farm group, however, there is a wide variation in incomes, with large commercial-type farmers receiving relatively high incomes and small farmers, especially in the South, receiving very low incomes. Since the majority of farmers fall in the low income group, the so-called farm problem is in considerable part a low income problem.

The incomes of small farmers are a combination of wages and profits (or losses). Many small farmers are unable to produce enough to provide reasonable incomes if prices of farm goods are set by the free play of market forces. Thus, since the 1930's, the federal government has consistently raised the price of major farm products above free market levels to assure farmers larger incomes than they would otherwise get. At these supported prices, farm production has exceeded the amounts consumers would buy, and this has led to large accumulations of surplus farm commodities by the government.

The "farm problem" should be understood broadly by students. It presents a good opportunity to use the simple tools outlined above to analyze a major national economic problem.

*The Desire for Economic Security*

Especially since the great depression of the 1930's, the American public has supported extensive steps to increase economic security through federal and state governmental action. Beyond direct government assistance to those obviously unable to take care of themselves, compulsory unemployment insurance is widespread, and federal old-age insurance now covers most of the population. These forms of economic security have been financed largely by payroll taxes on employers and workers, but partly out of general government funds. Parallel private steps to lessen insecurity have become increasingly prominent, both on an individual basis and through labor-management bargaining. Life insurance and retirement programs have grown very rapidly, involving huge pension fund accumulations. Private health insurance now covers a large portion of the population.

Students should be generally familiar with these various arrangements that directly affect their personal economic security. They should also be able to reason objectively about the economic effects, and hence the desirability from different points of view, of these different types of security measures. Should unemployment compensation benefits, for example, be paid to unemployed workers for longer periods than is now the case? Here the answer will depend partly on the ranking of goals. Is increased purchasing power to stimulate recovery most important? Or providing bare minimum living standards for unemployed workers? Or maintaining the unemployment insurance program on a continuously solvent actuarial basis? Similarly, the answer will depend partly on judgments about the effects of alternative measures—for example, would continued unemployment insurance payments substantially help to stimulate total spending and recovery?

The same approach can be taken to private pension plans, from which workers frequently do not derive maximum benefits unless they remain in a single company's employ. What are the goals? Do such plans seriously reduce the ability of workers to move to new jobs when they wish to do so? Should old-age insurance benefits be increased, and what would be the cost of doing so? Who should give up the goods and services used by the aged?

Some observers believe that governmental steps toward providing greater economic security have lessened our rate of economic growth and have moved the United States far toward becoming a "welfare state." They argue that such steps reduce both total current output and the incentive to work. Others argue that these programs increase the rate of economic growth, particularly when total spending is not rising rapidly enough, by providing more purchasing power to low income consumers. This stresses the possible conflict between the social goals of security and economic growth. But governmental action to lessen economic insecurity is still less in the United States than in most western industrialized nations, and is far less than the role of government in the socialist and communist countries.

---

## Essential Concepts and Institutions Introduced in This Section

In this section the following new essential concepts and economic institutions have been introduced:

Incomes as payments for productive services—productivity as a basis for receipt of incomes

Personal distribution of income

Real and money wages

Labor unions—collective bargaining

Strikes, picketing, closed shop, featherbedding

Economic security as a goal

Social security, unemployment insurance, old-age insurance, private security measures

The "farm problem"

In addition, many essential concepts from the earlier sections, such as supply and demand, have been re-used.

---

# Communism, Socialism, and Capitalism[1]

*Every informed American should have a general impression of how other types of economic systems operate, especially communism. Fear of dealing with controversial subjects should not be permitted to exclude objective discussion of this topic from the classroom.*

Different economic systems solve the major economic questions (what and how, how much, and for whom) in different ways. The world now includes economic systems which range over the spectrum from primary reliance on private enterprise through varying degrees of government ownership of productive resources (socialism) to the Russian and Chinese brands of communism (which are also forms of socialism but of a highly authoritarian kind). Along the spectrum different economies represent widely varying economic characteristics.

Students should be able to make an intelligent comparison between a private enterprise economy and a communist economy of the Russian type. Some of the most significant differences are noneconomic—political and social. But excluding questions of political freedom and other important noneconomic considerations, the economic comparison should include at least the following:

*The allocation of resources in a communist society is determined basically by the central planners, not by free consumer demands.* While consumers may be free to buy whatever is available in the market, the supply of consumer goods is determined by the central plan, and prices are set by the planners to assure the desired distribution of goods and services. Under communism, high priority has been given to capital accumulation and economic growth and to military preparation. The actual allocation of resources is controlled at all stages by an elaborate central plan, in contrast to the working of relatively free markets in the American economy.

*Individual economic incentives in the communist societies do not differ greatly from those in the American economy.* Originally, communist doctrine implied "from each according to his ability, to each according to his need." As a practical matter, the communist economies have found that money income provides one of the most effective incentives, and substantial differences in wages and salaries are used by the communists to draw workers into those areas where they are most

---

[1] This brief section involves examination of all three of the big economic questions raised in the three preceding sections.

needed and to obtain more and better work from them. Communist managers are rewarded, in effect, for efficient production in much the same way as American managers are, though without the American possibility of substantial capital accumulation by individuals. Thus to a considerable extent Russia has been forced to use the same pecuniary incentives (except notably in the case of incentives to capital) as do private enterprise economies.

*In the communist society nearly all capital goods and natural resources are owned by the state.* With only minor exceptions, the earnings of capital which go to private owners in a private enterprise economy are appropriated directly by the state in a communist economy. In effect, the government is free to set prices and wages so that the proceeds from its sale of goods to consumers, plus taxes, yield whatever excess over wage payments the government wishes to spend —either on direct services to citizens or on capital accumulation and military expenditures. While interest and profits are not a significant source of income to individuals in Russia, state officials find it necessary to engage in "profit calculations" in allocating resources to various industries and in determining in what directions to invest the capital being accumulated by the state.

*A major difference between the communist and private enterprise economies in recent years has been in the importance attached to capital accumulation and the rate of economic growth.* The communist economies, though much poorer than the United States, have chosen to allocate a large portion of their productive resources to capital accumulation and military expenditures. Many private enterprise economies, allowing freer play to individual choices, have allocated a smaller portion of their resources to capital accumulation and have grown more slowly.

*Communist societies have not suffered from economic instability (booms and depressions) to the same extent that private enterprise economies have.* This is partly because of the extent to which all communist economic activities are controlled by central planning, but especially because decisions on capital investment are made directly by the state, thus avoiding the instability of profit-motivated investment which characterizes private enterprise economies.

*In perspective, private enterprise economies have been much more successful than any other type in raising standards of living.* But communist economies have worked more effectively than many observers originally thought possible, and communism and capitalism are viewed today as active alternatives by most of the underdeveloped economies.

In addition to being able to compare private enterprise and communism, the student should also be sensitively aware of the fact that various democratic societies—the United Kingdom, the Scandinavian countries, and India, for example—have chosen to adopt socialism in varying degrees. This means that these countries prefer to have a larger fraction of their economic resources under government ownership and control than we have. This does not mean that these countries are any the less democratic in their form of government or that they are any the less friendly toward the United States. Here again there needs to be dispassionate analysis of the facts, and also recognition that different peoples, with their differing value systems, choose to organize their economies in different ways.

# FOUR

## *Recommendations*

The two preceding chapters outlined the minimum economic understanding essential for good citizenship and attainable by high school students. They emphasized that this requires not only a knowledge of important facts about the economy and its institutions, but also a rational, objective way of thinking about economic issues, and certain concepts and analytical tools to help in this thinking. We turn now to the question of how such an understanding can be achieved. This requires comments on the curriculum, approach and method, teachers, teaching materials, and controversial issues.

We offer a number of specific suggestions in this chapter, emphasizing, however, that they are meant to be suggestive and illustrative, not blueprints for universal adoption. We recognize, for example, that school authorities must weigh the curriculum changes that we suggest against many competing demands. Students vary widely in ability. Some schools have teachers well trained in economics; others do not. Moreover, those charged with responsibility for creating and using specific teaching methods and materials may often be able to improve upon those suggested below. We hope, however, that the general guidelines proposed here will be helpful to those charged with this important task.

### The Curriculum

1. *We recommend that more time be devoted in high school curricula to the development of economic understanding.* It is unrealistic to hope that most students will learn to think effectively about economic issues and to understand the functioning of the American economy without a substantial increase in the time devoted to this purpose in high school curricula. Economic understanding may be taught in separate courses in economics. It may be taught in other courses dealing with economic institutions and issues. How it is most effectively taught will, of course, depend on the students involved, the preparation of the teachers, the amount of time available, and other

such conditions. But more time and serious attention, focused along the lines outlined in Chapters II and III, are required in most schools if anything approaching the minimal competence indicated there is to be attained by most students.

In the following sections we indicate our recommendations, depending upon the amount of student time that local school boards and administrators choose to devote to economics in their curricula.

*Courses in Economics*

2. *We recommend that wherever feasible students take a high school course in economics or its equivalent under another title (such as Problems of American Democracy); and that in all high schools of substantial size there be at least an elective senior-year course in economics.* To attain the level of economic understanding suggested above will require at least a full semester course for high school students. For most students, even a full course may prove insufficient unless a preliminary groundwork has been laid in earlier courses, introducing both economic institutions and a logical, objective way of thinking about social problems. Thus, we believe that the equivalent of a one semester course is necessary, but not sufficient for most students, to assure the minimum level of economic understanding we recommend.

We recognize the many competing demands on the high school curriculum. Each school board, of course, must decide in view of its circumstances whether or not to *require* a separate course in economics of all its students. We see no practical alternative to assure that all high school graduates attain something like the level of understanding indicated above.[1] Where no such course is required, we do urge that it should, at a minimum, be available as an elective in all schools of substantial size.

---

[1] For the minority of students going on to college and already sure they will take a college course in economics, it may be desirable to take instead further high school work in mathematics, advanced English composition, or some comparable foundation course. But even for these students some degree of repetitive learning between high school and college economics may be advantageous. Most subjects are not thoroughly learned the first time they are studied. Moreover, as more students come to college with a minimal understanding of economic institutions and processes the level and effectiveness of college courses in economics can be raised as has been the case in physics, chemistry, and mathematics in recent years.

While we recommend no particular course arrangement or teaching approach in such a course, we do urge that stress be placed on objective, careful reasoning about economic problems (as we suggest in Chapter II), on understanding the over-all functioning of the economy and on the major problem areas, institutions, and analytical concepts outlined in Chapter III. We warn against the superficial description that appears to characterize so many present high school courses, and against teaching that stresses memorization of trivial facts, dates, and unused lists of concepts. Such information is soon forgotten, and courses of this sort have little claim to the serious high school student's time.

### Economics in Problems of American Democracy Courses

3. *We recommend that courses in problems of American democracy (now taken by perhaps half of all high school students) devote a substantial portion of their time to development of economic understanding of the kind outlined in Chapters II and III above.* Such courses usually cover a variety of problems, or problem areas, like social security, international relations, big business, conservation of natural resources, public finance, and agriculture. Since the course employs the "problem approach," it can afford excellent training in economic reasoning. On each problem studied, teachers can show that rational decision-making must be based not on ignorance and prejudice but on a careful process of understanding the relevant facts, of analyzing the forces that produce the "problem," of clarifying goals, and of choosing carefully among the available alternatives. Some of the essential concepts and analytical tools outlined in Chapter III can be developed in connection with each problem area.

For example, the "farm problem" leads readily to analysis of demand and supply as they interact in the market to establish prices, and to the role of markets in channeling productive resources to meet consumer demands. Government policies to deal with low farm incomes and farm surpluses pose the need to define the economic problem to be solved and the social goals to be achieved, then to list the main alternative courses of action, to evaluate the consequences of these courses, and finally, to choose the alternative which promises best to achieve the desired goals. Teaching materials for such an approach could include readings on the changing political and economic role of the farmer, data on farm incomes and living standards compared to other groups, information and conflicting views on the values of rural vs. urban living, and recent proposals for "solving" the farm problem through alternative governmental policies—in addition to the analytical materials on supply, demand, prices, and markets suggested above. Economic concepts and principles will have meaning for most students only as they are applied to concrete problems and situations.

Similarly, consideration of monopoly and big business can lead into analysis of the nature of a basically private enterprise economy; the role of competition in markets for products and for labor; the effects of monopoly power on output, prices, and incomes; and the problems of achieving simultaneously reasonable competition and low-cost mass production. The topic of comparative economic systems offers a challenging opportunity to emphasize that all types of economies must somehow deal with the three big economic problems (what, how much, and for whom), and then to compare and contrast their objectives and the methods, institutions, and incentives they employ to achieve them. We have suggested one approach for handling this area in the closing section of Chapter III.

Introduction of more economic analysis into problems of American democracy courses can help significantly to develop the economic understanding needed for good citizenship, if it is done with the objectives and flavor indicated above. We repeat that mere description of facts, institutions and situations accomplishes little of lasting value. Analytically oriented teaching materials, competent teaching, and specific focus on the goals of developing economic understanding and ability to reason independently, are all required if problems of American democracy courses are to contribute significantly to economic understanding.

*Economics in History Courses*

4. *We recommend that more economic analysis be included in history courses.* Almost all students take an American history course in the eleventh grade or in a two-year sequence through the twelfth grade. This course presents excellent opportunities for deepening economic understanding and for adding a new dimension to history itself. It inevitably deals with many economic events—tariffs, banking controversies, inflation and deflation, the rise of large-scale business, growth of labor unions, the growing role of government in economic affairs,

and many more. If such problems are considered analytically as well as merely descriptively and chronologically, great numbers of high school students will gain in both economic understanding and historical perspective.

American history courses often attempt to cover the entire sweep of American political and social history including attention to developments in many facets of American life. Moreover, they customarily stress chronology rather than an analytical approach to particular elements of historical development, such as the specific economic problems indicated above. Lastly, historians themselves are understandably often concerned with teaching an historical discipline itself as a major goal in such a course.

Thus, to introduce emphasis on economic understanding along the line we suggest will require, for most history courses, significant changes in approach, materials, and teaching method. We nevertheless urge that this be done, since for many students this is the only formal exposure in the high school curriculum to economic institutions and problems. Special units of economics, in addition to the usual descriptive materials on economic events, could introduce students to the elements of economic reasoning. Such units could easily be developed by economists and historians working together, as we recommend below.

To illustrate, agricultural developments during the last century could readily be taught along the lines indicated above for the problems in American democracy course, by allocating some extra time and using appropriate supplementary readings. Another illustration is provided by the great depression of the 1930's. Most American history texts deal with this descriptively, with primary attention to political developments and the legislation of the New Deal, but little attention to the underlying economic forces involved, analysis of the social goals sought or effectiveness of such legislation.

To supplement this usual historical treatment, economic materials could readily be introduced showing the similarity of the basic economic developments of the 1930's to earlier depressions, and introducing a few of the simple economic concepts noted in Chapter III—for example, gross national product, money and real income, aggregate demand (spending) and its major components. A simple analysis could be introduced stressing the shortage of aggregate demand in the depression, and the relation of monetary contraction between 1929 and 1933 to this demand shortage and to falling prices. Against this background, students could be led to consider government policies to stimulate recovery through monetary expansion and budgetary policy as well as through direct measures (like NRA and AAA). While the analysis would need to be very elementary, at least students could be led to see the elements of economic reasoning, along the lines outlined in Chapter II, and could be introduced to a few of the central economic institutions and concepts outlined in the second major section of Chapter III.

Numerous other possibilities for such units exist—for example, the post-Civil War inflation and monetary collapse, the Sherman Act and its relation to the monopoly problem, and the continuing tariff controversy.

It would be unrealistic to expect that the economic understanding needed for good citizenship can be achieved through American history courses alone. But such courses can make a worth-wile contribution, especially if they can build on earlier attention to economic institutions and if appropriate teaching materials are used to supplement the basic history texts.

Similar economic units could be introduced into world history courses, which typically concentrate on political and social developments. For example, comparative rates of growth in output and living standards of different nations provide a vital issue around which a unit designed to develop economic understanding can readily be built. Focus on natural resources, technology, education, labor force, form of economic organization, and other factors underlying economic growth could introduce these fundamental concepts. Data showing comparative growth rates for highly developed and underdeveloped nations could illustrate the importance of saving and capital accumulation and, at the same time, point up the different factors influencing these rates in different economies—for example, the private enterprise and the communist varieties. Consideration could also be given in this connection to the origins and development of capitalism, and the causes and significance of the industrial revolution.

Increased emphasis on development of economic understanding need not detract from the importance attached to other forces in historical development. Indeed, it can be used to enrich students' understanding of history. For this subject provides a broad framework for the understanding of social, political, and economic forces, within which increased stress on an analytical approach to economic developments can contribute to both historical and economic understanding.

*Economics in Business Education*

5. *We recommend that all business education curricula include a required course in economics.* A large group of high school students take special studies intended to prepare them for careers in business. These curricula include bookkeeping, typing, office practice, and a variety of other courses focused on current business practice. Since few of these students go on to college, we especially urge that all such curricula include a course in economics, similar to the one outlined in recommendation No. 2 above.

Minimal training in economics for these students is justified on both citizenship and career training grounds. While the high school course in economics should not be focused on business operations or personal finance, a reasonable acquaintance with basic economic institutions will prove valuable for any student entering a business firm. Moreover, many teachers in the business education curriculum have had at least one college course in economics, since this is required for teacher certification much more commonly than for teachers in the social studies.

Business education also provides other places for developing economic understanding. For example, bookkeeping courses can be given much more intellectual content by relating them to simple business accounting concepts, to the role of costs and profits in business firms, and to such concepts as gross national product and national income.

*Other Opportunities*

6. *We recommend that economic understanding be emphasized at several other points in the entire school curriculum.* There are many opportunities for building economic understanding from the time the child enters first grade until he graduates from high school. Interesting experiments now under way suggest that such simple notions as division of labor, prices, exchange in markets, and even profit can be grasped by elementary school children if they are built into carefully planned teaching materials and methods. Inescapably, children are exposed to such ideas in their day-to-day lives. The elementary grades provide an opportunity to clarify them, and to relate them to daily problems of family living, especially in the social studies courses children take from the early grades. We commend these experiments

and recommend adoption of these techniques in the earlier grades as this becomes feasible.

Geography courses, included in all curricula, provide excellent opportunities to relate the usual descriptive materials to the role of such factors as natural resources, climate, and transportation facilities to the basic economic processes of specialization and exchange. Discussion of differing rates of economic growth in relation to varying possession of natural resources can provide a lively focus for the importance of geography. So can analysis of the geographical bases for the location of different industries. Introduction of such economic issues can help to enliven courses that often become routine.

Mathematics courses offer special promise for introducing students to precise reasoning about economic problems. Although arithmetic and algebra courses typically include problems in personal finance and in business arithmetic, they could equally include use of other economic problems and concepts. For example, supply and demand curves could be employed to illustrate simple graphs. Simple relationships between income and consumption could illustrate the use of linear equations in elementary algebra. We urge teachers and textbook writers to include more such examples, and professional economists to help provide them.

Civics courses, usually taught in the ninth grade, touch at many points on economic issues and problems. Courses in home economics offer opportunities to discuss such things as the role of the consumer, personal saving, and social security in the American economy. Curriculum planners, textbook writers, and teachers in all these courses can do much to provide a foundation for the economic understanding that should be a direct focus of academic work for most students in the final years of high school work. We believe that introduction of more economic materials and concepts need not detract from the educational value of these other courses, but can instead enliven and enrich them.

## Approaches to Teaching

7. *We recommend central emphasis on the rational way of thinking presented in Chapter II as a prime objective of the teaching of economics.* We are not competent to advise in detail how teachers in the schools might best develop in their widely differing students the economic understanding we suggest as needed for good citizenship. The

most effective approaches and methods will vary depending on the course, teacher, and students involved. But we believe it is far more important for students to learn to think about economic situations objectively and rationally for themselves than to learn masses of institutional details, or memorize lists of unused economic concepts. Many students, perhaps most, will learn less economics than the minimum outlined in Chapter III. What they do study, however, should be studied analytically and in reasonable depth, rather than as superficial memory work. A rational way of thinking about economic problems is the first step toward economic understanding.

For students of all ability levels, it is important to establish courses of rigor and challenge comparable to those now offered in science and mathematics. There is research evidence to substantiate the claim that analysis is beneficial to everyone, not merely to those of high ability. It is true that students of high ability can be expected to learn more in less time. But this should not mean analysis for the bright and mere memorization for the less able, though for them a greater stress on facts and institutions will generally be realistic. To aid teachers, we have indicated throughout Chapter III some of the areas and concepts which are likely to prove too difficult for lower ability students.

We wish to re-emphasize here that "objectivity" in economics does not mean merely giving equal time and attention to all competing biases. Rather it means thinking through the situation with clear recognition of the alternative assumptions being made in competing arguments. "Objectivity" implies rational analysis. It does not mean giving students the idea that any view or answer is as good as another.

Lastly, we urge that teachers emphasize getting students to *use* the economic concepts they are asked to learn. Supply and demand means little unless the student sees how he can use them in understanding why farm surpluses persist in the face of government price support policies, or in studying other such practical issues. Saving has meaning when he sees what it means for the family and the local business firm as well as for the economy as a whole. Gross national product is merely a set of technical words unless he sees how it helps him to measure the comparative performance of the American and Russian economies. These are only examples, but they suggest the importance of stressing student use of economic concepts in analyzing practical problems, and the importance of giving the concepts and institutions taught concrete meaning in relation to the student's own experience and interests.

## Controversial Issues

8. *We recommend that examination of controversial issues be included, where appropriate, in teaching economics.* Economic understanding and objective analysis cannot be developed in the schools if controversial issues are eliminated from consideration. The more important the economic issue, the more controversial is it likely to be. To avoid issues because they are controversial or to limit serious discussion of them will not make the problems go away or contribute to their rational solution. It will only invite decisions based on ignorance, prejudice, and passion.

The very nature of democracy implies serious discussion by the people. Limitations on discussion of important public problems are not merely infringements on the rights of teachers to teach. More important, they are infringements on the rights of students to learn, to think, and to arrive at their own conclusions. They are thus a threat to the quality of future citizens and to the success of democracy itself.

In approaching controversial issues, teachers should be responsible for leading students to use the analytical, objective approach described earlier—get the relevant facts; clarify objectives; identify, analyze, and compare the various alternative courses of action; and choose among the alternatives in light of the objectives sought. In this process students will inevitably be exposed to points of view not shared by some parents and other groups in the community. They will also subject to critical analysis some points of view to which their parents and others may be devoted. It is not to be expected that such searching analysis will be universally welcomed. But to deprive students of the opportunity to think through controversial issues for themselves is to deprive them of fundamental training for good citizenship and to deny the fundamental tenets of a free and democratic society. To insist upon and defend this right of the teacher and of the students is the duty of every citizen, as well as of teachers, administrators, and school boards, even when particular groups criticize the teacher involved. Ours is a strong society which need not fear open discussion of its economic institutions and processes.

## Teachers

9. *To improve the ability of teachers, we recommend several steps.* Obviously, economic understanding cannot be imparted by teachers who do not themselves understand economics. As we pointed out in

Chapter I, apparently almost half of all high school social studies teachers, and perhaps a quarter of all those teaching actual courses in economics, have not had as much as a single college course in economics. This is intolerable if we want their students to develop real economic understanding. It would be equally futile to expect teachers who had never had a college course in mathematics or physics to teach mathematics or physics effectively.

Most teachers try sincerely to do a good job. They work hard to obtain better materials for their courses and to improve their own abilities. The need is to provide more effective ways to help present teachers improve their own understanding, to provide better teaching aids and materials, and to be sure that new teachers obtain the needed preparation in economics during their college years. Thus:

(a) *We recommend that teacher certification requirements in all states require a minimum of one full year (6 unit) course in college economics for all social studies and business education teachers.* An elementary understanding of the way our economic system functions, and of economic reasoning, is a minimum basis for reasonable teaching of economics in history, problems of American democracy, and all other such social studies and business courses in which economics has a logical place. At least another year of college economics beyond the elementary course would be highly desirable.

(b) *We recommend that school boards and administrators consider these certification standards as minimum requirements, and they take steps to enforce higher standards wherever feasible.* For instructors who teach specific courses in economics we recommend, wherever feasible, at least a college minor in economics (usually about 18 units), and preferably a college major in the field. Short of a college minor, the high school teacher of economics has formal training that puts him only a small margin ahead of his best students. This is not the way to obtain teaching that stretches the minds of high school youths and leads them to thorough understanding. While small school systems may be unable to afford such a trained economist, every large school system should have at least one such person on its social studies staff, both to teach its courses in economics and, equally important, to help other teachers in selecting materials and teaching approaches where economic issues are involved.

(c) *To help present teachers improve their economic competence, we recommend increased use of summer workshops, teacher participa-*

*tion in a nationwide television economics course planned for 1962-63, and return to college for additional work in economics.* School authorities should encourage and assist teachers to improve their economic understanding through all these channels, including, wherever feasible, provision of financial support for further training. Summer workshops for high school teachers are available in most states through the Joint Council on Economic Education. During the 1962-63 school year, a special television program on the American economy will be presented nationwide daily, to help all interested high school teachers obtain a reasonable grasp of the functioning of the economy. It will also offer suggestions as to how economic understanding can be woven into history and problems of American democracy courses, as well as taught in courses in economics. This Learning Resources Institute television course, co-sponsored by the American Economic Association and the Joint Council on Economic Education and under the guidance of a group of distinguished economists and educators, will emphasize the approach to economic understanding outlined in the preceding chapters, and will involve many of the nation's outstanding economists and educators as teachers.

(d) *We recommend that colleges preparing teachers improve the economics courses offered for this purpose, and establish other opportunities for high school teachers to increase their economic understanding.* Colleges can help by designing improved courses in basic economics specifically for high school teachers which emphasize the kind of economic competence outlined in Chapters II and III. In many institutions, this will require a substantial change in the emphasis and direction of basic courses in economics. These colleges can also help by designing extension courses for teachers along similar lines. Furthermore, we recommend that more colleges and universities offer summer workshops in economics for high school teachers. All too often, leading university economists pay little attention to this pressing problem of secondary school teaching. Finally, we commend the establishment of university centers for economic education such as those of Iowa, Illinois, and Purdue, which focus on research and aid to the teaching of economics in the schools.

### Teaching Materials

10. *We emphasize the need for more effective high school teaching materials and recommend that steps be taken by private publishers,*

223

*foundations, and others to increase the supply of such materials.* Better teaching materials are essential if the minimal level of economic understanding described above is to be achieved by most students in the high schools.

As we pointed out in Chapter I, better texts are beginning to appear, but too frequently the textbooks on economics used in the schools are prosaic and uninteresting. They are devoted largely to facts and descriptions unrelated to major current public problems, lacking in careful analysis, and full of policy prescriptions based largely on the unsupported views of the authors. Materials on economics in problems of American democracy and history texts suffer from the same failings, when, indeed, any pretense of dealing with economic issues is included. The supplementary materials that pour in on social studies teachers from many different groups like business, labor, and farm organizations range from the objective and informative to sheer propaganda. Far too much of such materials falls close to the latter extreme. Most high school teachers have neither the time nor the training to sift through all this to choose what would be effective in the classroom. Thus, major steps are needed to provide better teaching materials. Better high school texts on economics and means to help teachers select from among the flood of supplementary materials available are required for all except the most sophisticated instructors.

Good teaching materials should be made generally available at modest cost if they are to be widely used. They are needed perhaps even more for problems of American democracy and history courses than for courses in economics, for almost none of the present materials for those courses appear to be aimed at developing the kind of economic understanding we urge for effective citizenship. Such materials need to be prepared as practical units for insertion into problems of American democracy and American and world history courses without the complete restructuring of such sourses, for they have other important objectives as well. Joint work by economists, historians, sociologists, and political scientists will be required in producing the needed materials. As a specific example, we suggest that the Joint Council on Economic Education and the Service Center for Teachers of History cooperate in developing guides to teachers wishing to incorporate more economic analysis into history courses.

Some steps in this direction have already been taken. A group of teachers and economists has sifted through the great mass of mate-

224

rials on "economics" already available with a view to selecting, recommending, and making available to teachers and students those that are most objective and most useful in promoting the desired economic understanding. The Joint Council on Economic Education is assisting in the preparation of new materials to the same end. More competent professional economists are becoming interested in preparing materials for the secondary schools, and some publishers are considering publication of textbooks and supplementary materials better suited to this purpose. We commend these efforts, and urge support by businesses, private citizens, professional economists, foundations, and government agencies for steps to provide teachers and students with the very best materials for developing economic understanding. We hope that the suggestions in Chapters II and III above may prove helpful to those interested in preparing new materials for high school courses and to teachers in deciding what materials can contribute most.

## The Responsibility of Economists

11. *We recommend that professional economists play a more active part in helping to raise the level of economics in the schools.* Leading economists have generally paid little attention to the teaching of economics below the college level. We consider this unfortunate. Professional economists can help significantly by assisting local teachers and school authorities in revising courses and curricula, by aiding in the preparation of more effective teaching materials, by supporting college courses for high school teachers designed to develop economic understanding of the sort described above, and by participating more actively in summer workshops and other special aids to high school teachers, arranged by the Joint Council on Economic Education or other responsible agencies. We urge our fellow economists to participate more actively in all of these ways to help improve the teaching of economics in the schools. To fail to do so is to shirk an important professional responsibility.

## Public Support

12. *We urge widespread public support, both private and governmental, for the improvement of economics in the schools.* Only if the leaders of public opinion, and the public itself, support higher standards for economic understanding in the schools will significant improvement occur. Community leaders need to give active support to teachers,

225

administrators and school boards seeking to raise standards—and to push school officials where this is needed. In doing so, they must recognize that economic understanding rests on a good grasp of economic institutions and an orderly way of thinking about economic issues, not an acceptance of some particular group interest or some "brand" of economics.

Many of the suggestions made above will cost money, though some can be achieved within present school budgets. Most of the cost of better education must ultimately be borne by the taxpayers and others who now support the schools. In lifting standards of economic understanding during the years immediately ahead, however, we urge special support, both governmental and private, for measures like those recommended above to speed this improvement.

*The following individuals provided assistance
through reading and review
at various stages of the Task Force's work:*

Dr. Albert Alexander
*Economic Education Coordinator*
*New York City Public Schools*

Prof. James D. Calderwood
*School of Business Administration*
*University of Southern California*

Prof. Harold Clark
*Professor of Education*
*Teachers College*
*Columbia University*

Mr. Shirley Cooper
*American Assn. of School Administrators*

Dr. Howard H. Cummings
*Office of Education*
*U. S. Dept. of Health,*
*Education & Welfare*

Prof. Edgar Edwards, *Chairman*
*Department of Economics*
*Rice Institute*

Dr. Finis Engleman, *Executive Secretary*
*American Assn. of School Administrators*

Dr. Martin Essex
*Superintendent of Schools*
*Akron Public Schools*

Dr. Helen M. Flynn
*Director of Secondary Instruction*
*Great Neck Public Schools*

Mr. Edgar Fuller, *Executive Secretary*
*Chief State School Officers Association*

Dr. Margaret Gill, *Executive Secretary*
*Association for Supervision of Secondary*
*   School Principals*

Dr. Hollis P. Guy, *Executive Secretary*
*United Business Education Association*

Mr. Merrill Hartshorn
*Executive Secretary*
*National Council for the Social Studies*

Prof. Herbert Heaton
*Department of History*
*Johns Hopkins University*

Dr. Theral T. Herrick, *Director*
*Department of Instruction & Guidance*
*Kalamazoo Public Schools*

Dr. Eunice Johns, *Chairman*
*Dept. of Social Studies*
*Wilmington Public Schools*

Prof. Earl S. Johnson
*School of Education*
*University of Wisconsin*

Dr. John D. Lawrence, *Director*
*Division of Secondary Education*
*Los Angeles County Schools*

Dr. Richard Miller, *Associate Director*
*Project on Instruction in*
*Elementary and Secondary Schools*

Prof. G. Shorey Peterson
*Department of Economics*
*University of Michigan*

Prof. Jim E. Reese
*Department of Economics*
*University of Oklahoma*

Dr. Ole Sand, *Director*
*Project on Instruction in*
*Elementary and Secondary Schools*

Prof. Philip E. Taylor, *Head*
*Department of Economics*
*University of Connecticut*

Dr. Ellsworth Tompkins
*Executive Secretary*
*National Council for the Social Studies*

Prof. Lewis E. Wagner
*Department of Economics*
*University of Illinois*

Report of the National Task Force on Economic Education, © Committee for
Economic Development, New York, 1961. Reprinted by permission of publisher.

227

## DATE DUE